THE
KRIEGSMARINE

A COLLECTOR'S GUIDE TO

THE
KRIEGSMARINE

CHRISTOPHER J. AILSBY

Ian Allan
PUBLISHING

First published 2007

ISBN (10) 0 7110 3099 5
ISBN (13) 978 9 7110 3099 2

Published by Ian Allan Publishing

an imprint of Ian Allan Publishing Ltd,
Hersham, Surrey KT12 4RG.
Printed in England by Ian Allan Printing
Ltd, Hersham, Surrey KT12 4RG.

Code: 0710/C

Visit the Ian Allan Publishing website at
www.ianallanpublishing.com

Dedicated to
Jason and Rebecca Elmore

Front cover, main: Naval officer wearing the
Officer of the Watch badge.

Front cover, bottom left: High Seas Fleet War
Badge.

Front cover, bottom middle: Badge for the entrance
of the Torp.Kdo.Danzig.

Front cover, bottom right: Auxiliary Cruisers War
Badge.

Back cover: The death citation for a lost U-boat
serviceman.

Picture credits:

Contents

Introduction 6

Cap Tallies 8

Rank Insignia 10

Rank Badges 10

Career Insignia of Seamen 11

Rank Insignia of Junior Non-Commissioned Officers 20

Warrant Officers' Rank and Career Badges 21

Career Insignia for Cadets 32

Commissioned Officers' Rank Badges 34

Career Insignia of Officers 35

Duty Badges 40

Sleeve Badges of Specialists 43

Spanish Civil War Awards 49

Cuff Titles 66

Arm Shields Common to all Services 70

Naval Decorations, Medals and Award Badges 1933-45 82

Naval War Badges 1939–45 87

LDO Numbers 149

Introduction

The origins of a German navy can be traced to the end of the Napoleonic Wars in 1815, following which Prussia and the other German states began to draw together into trade areas or custom unions, known as Zollverein. However, at that time and for some years after, most of the German states were totally land-oriented and had little feeling for naval matters – so much so that the German merchant fleets, which plied mainly from the Baltic coast and Hamburg, could be threatened by a navy as small as Denmark's.

In 1848 a combined German States Navy came into existence under the name of Reich Marine, but due to an inability to coordinate diplomatic aspirations between the states, the infant Reich Marine was abolished in 1852. However, the Royal Prussian Navy stayed in existence and would form the basis of the navy of Germany in later years. The 'Iron Chancellor', Otto von Bismarck, realised the necessity for a strong navy and it was he who was to become the father of that navy. He introduced modern 'ironclad' ships in the 1870s, beginning a process of naval expansion, which angered Britain and worsened relations between the two countries from the 1880s onwards.

Continuing naval rivalry between Britain and Germany, in European waters, and in colonial areas around the world played a significant part in bringing about World War 1. Before that time most naval authorities thought that the decisive actions of a major war would be fought by the great battleship fleets but it was not to be. After the German surface fleet was sent scurrying back to port in the 1916 Battle of Jutland, Germany turned to a new weapon: the submarine or U-boat. The U-boat campaign was duly defeated in 1917-18 but not before it had become clear that the nature of naval warfare had changed. The capital ships that until that time had been invincible were now under threat; naval strategy had to be rethought.

With the Versailles Treaty of 1919, Britain inflicted a crushing blow on the German Navy.

It was to be reduced to a fraction of its former size; it was to have no modern battleships and no submarines. The largest part of the German Navy had surrendered and was interned at the main British fleet base at Scapa Flow. The ships were left to swing at their moorings, manned by skeleton crews, awaiting their fate. Finally, angered by the progress of the peace negotiations, the German admirals decided to regain pride and honour by scuttling the whole fleet at its moorings in the anchorage.

Even before Adolf Hitler came to power in 1933, the German Navy was reconstructed under the Weimar Republic. Hitler continued and accelerated the process. On 16 March 1935, he repudiated the disarmament clauses of the Treaty of Versailles, reintroduced military conscription, and announced the creation of a German air force and other measures in direct contravention of the Treaty. On 21 May 1935, the German Navy, known as the Reichsmarine under the Weimar Republic, was renamed the Kriegsmarine. Far from standing up against these moves, Britain then negotiated an Anglo-German Naval Agreement which permitted Germany to build and operate warships to a strength up to 35% of the British Royal Navy, and to develop a submarine force. Hitler told Admiral Erich Raeder, Commander-in-Chief of the German Navy, that the day the agreement was signed was the happiest of his life. Raeder himself told his officers they could not have hoped for better conditions during the coming decade.

Around this time Hitler informed Raeder that he would not precipitate a full-scale war until at least 1944. It was on this assumption that Raeder planned the German Navy's expansion. When war came in 1939, five years earlier than he had thought, many of the ships that Raeder had hoped would be in service were still being built, or were on the designer's drawing boards. Needless to say, Germany still had a formidable navy. The three pocket battleships begun by the Weimar Republic, which should have been 10,000 tons to keep within the regulations of the Treaty of 1919, had been secretly built to 13,000 tons and these were immediately available for any conflict. The later and larger battlecruisers *Scharnhorst* and *Gneisenau* were formidable adversaries for any navy to meet. The big *Hipper*-class cruisers, 4,000 tons over treaty weight, were nearly ready, and added to this impressive array were 56 U-boats. Their crews had been well trained, starting during the years when no U-boats were supposedly permitted. Admiral Karl Dönitz, who was to strengthen their fighting ability and to build the 'wolf pack' system of attack, ably led the U-boat flotillas.

Battle instructions were issued to the fleet in May 1939. The plan revolved round the idea of a continuous series of operations in the North Sea, to create as much havoc as possible by engaging in attacking the shipping in that area which, it was hoped, would involve large British forces to contain them. The larger ships were instructed to cruise in the oceans of the world in a heavy and sustained attack on the merchant marine of any allied nation.

The main aim of the U-boats was to operate against the convoys in the Atlantic and, especially, in the approaches to the main British ports. To offset the delay in the heavy ships still under production, it was decided that a number of merchant ships should be fitted out as auxiliary cruisers. In all there were nine raiders, of which the most successful was the *Pinguin*, which scored 28 sinkings, and then the *Atlantis* captained by Bernhard Rogge with a score of 22.

In the German battle instructions one ominous phrase was inserted, which was to bode badly for the naval commanders in later years: 'Fighting methods will never fail to be employed merely because some international regulations are opposed to them.' It was to foreshadow the unrestricted submarine and raider warfare that was to follow.

It was in this climate that the German Navy went to war and its personnel wore the insignia and earned the badges and medals described in this book. Finally, with the collapse of Germany, Admiral Raeder, who had overseen the expansion and rearmament of the German Navy and directed its operations until 1943, was sentenced at Nuremberg to life imprisonment. After Göring and Himmler fell from favour in April 1945, Dönitz (who had succeeded Raeder in command of the Kriegsmarine) was nominated by Hitler to succeed him as head of state. Dönitz became the last Führer and had the onerous task of arranging the surrender of Germany. He received a ten-year jail sentence at the Nuremberg Trials. His claim that he was purely a professional naval officer was partially believed by the court, which went a considerable way to reducing his sentence. This was a light sentence compared to the 90% fatality rate of the members of U-boat crews.

The end of the war did not see an end to all activities by the Kriegsmarine. In one bizarre incident two German naval deserters were executed by their countrymen several days after the surrender, in the Allied-occupied Netherlands, under the supervision of Canadian forces. In other areas German–Allied co-operation was more constructive. A joint British–German force was employed to clear mines from the Baltic from 1945 until 1947. This was led by Lieutenant-Commander Albert McRae, who, when he was relieved, was given a collection of naval insignia, badges and daggers which made up the brick library of the Kriegsmarine in Kiel, together with a silver salver which had the dates engraved surrounding the German naval flag. A great number of the illustrations in this book are taken from items in this collection.

Cap Tallies

Providing comprehensive coverage of cap tallies in a book of this size and scope would be impossible. Instead I have tried to outline the general principles of their use and deployment. In doing this I have chosen to detail a unique use of the pre-war style of tally on the *Prinz Eugen* after the conclusion of the war. A most interesting photo used later in the book shows the tally in wear in January 1946 together with the Naval Close Combat Clasp. I have included a short history of the ship to give an insight into the German Navy's capital ships as well as to show the use of the tally after the war.

Prior to the outbreak of war, cap tallies – which identified the ship, flotilla or land-based unit to which the wearer was assigned – were worn by junior NCOs and seamen around the sailor's cap. This had a rigid band with a floppy wide-brimmed top fitting over it. The colour was dark blue for winter, white for summer and for tropical waters. By the Navy Mobilisation Order dated 1 November 1938 a cap tally bearing the title 'Kriegsmarine' was introduced for general wear in case of mobilisation. Cap tallies with other titles were permitted for wear within barracks and on ships provided that there was absolute security. The wearers of these tallies were forbidden to have any contact with the outside world. A supplement to the Mobilisation Order, dated mid-1940, prohibited any further wearing of cap tallies with peacetime titles and required collection of the tallies. The only exceptions to this regulation were the tallies of NCO Preparatory Schools.

The heavy cruiser *Prinz Eugen*, the fourth warship to bear that name, was the third and last heavy cruiser commissioned by the Kriegsmarine. She was launched in 1938 as part of an ambitious peacetime building programme intended to bring the Kriegsmarine to equal terms with the Royal Navy. The *Prinz Eugen* was a magnificent ship by any measure; her elegant, purposeful design embodied both the cutting edge of German naval engineering, and the *esprit de corps* of the Kriegsmarine. But in 1941 she was commissioned into a fleet that had been poorly prepared for war, facing a vastly superior enemy. *Prinz Eugen* became famous on her first war mission in May 1941 during the Atlantic sortie with the ill-fated *Bismarck* which began so well, from the German point-of-view, when the *Hood* was sunk and the

Photo 1 Obverse of the cap tally issued on 5 January 1946 by the German office in charge. *John Robinson*

Photo 2 Reverse of cap tally. According to Gunnery Officer Paul Schmalenbach who served on the *Prinz Eugen* throughout the war, this cap tally was organised to strengthen the morale of the remaining 574 crewmembers. *John Robinson*

Photo 3 The German and US crews became friendly during the transit of the *Prinz Eugen* as is the nature of sailors. Such comradeship resulted in the exchanges of personal items such as sleeve insignias, cap badges and tallies, etc. Both sides knew that the *Prinz Eugen* was to be sunk by an atomic bomb in the Pacific Ocean – no reason to let rare items go to the bottom. *John Robinson*

Prince of Wales damaged. In February 1942, after a period spent in Brest, the *Prinz Eugen*, accompanied by the battlecruisers *Scharnhorst* and *Gneisenau*, successfully passed through the English Channel on the way back to Germany. The daring Channel Dash may have been a moral victory but it was no great contribution to the war effort. Shortly afterwards, while *en route* to Norway, *Prinz Eugen* was torpedoed by the British submarine *Trident* off Trondheim causing considerable damage to the stern. Emergency repairs kept her afloat and the heavy cruiser managed to limp back to Kiel under her own steam. She was in dock until October 1942. The ship was not ready for service until the beginning of 1943, and was then used in the Baltic for training purposes and as an experimental vessel for testing new apparatus and weapons.

On 15 October 1944, while travelling at 20 knots, she accidentally rammed the light cruiser *Leipzig*. With repairs complete, *Prinz Eugen's* finest hour came in March 1945, when she was deployed for shore bombardment off the Baltic coast against the advancing Soviet troops to cover the evacuation of refugees. Her shells held back the onrushing Red Army units, allowing a mass German exodus. On 10 April 1945, she left Swinemünde on the Baltic for Copenhagen where she arrived on the 20th. *Prinz Eugen* and the light cruiser *Nürnberg* surrendered to British forces at Copenhagen on 7 May 1945.

The *Prinz Eugen* was handed over to the Americans on 5 January 1946. The American flag was hoisted and the ship put into service in the US Navy as USS *Prinz Eugen* (IX-300). The German senior officer of the small crew made available to assist the US Navy to set sail for America decided to raise the morale of his men by issuing them cap tallies. These bore the title 'Prinz Eugen'. It is estimated that 150 or so of the tallies were issued. These named tallies were probably stored in the ship, as these named tallies had been used prior to the war. The *Prinz Eugen*, with a mixed crew of Germans and Americans, set sail for Boston on 13 January 1946 arriving nine days later. From there she was moved to Philadelphia shortly after, where the barrels of turret 'Anton' were removed.

In March 1946 she left for the Pacific through the Panama Canal. The last German crew members left the ship in San Diego on 1 May 1946. Her next destination was Bikini Atoll in the Marshall Islands. At 09.00, on 1 July 1946, A-bomb test Able took place. A nuclear bomb was dropped over a target fleet of ships by a B-29 and detonated at 518 feet above the surface. The *Prinz Eugen* was located 1,194 yards from the point of explosion and survived the test undamaged. A second A-bomb test was undertaken on 25 July 1946. A nuclear bomb was detonated underwater at a depth of about 90 feet. The *Prinz Eugen* was 1,990 yards from the explosion, and survived this test too, without appreciable damage. She was later towed to Kwajalein Atoll, where leaks caused her to take on a 35-degree starboard list. She capsized on Enubuj reef on 22 December 1946.

Prinz Eugen never sank a single enemy vessel, but her crew fondly remembered her as a lucky ship. Although heavily damaged on several occasions, *Prinz Eugen* was the only large surface unit of the Kriegsmarine to survive World War 2 intact. Under the circumstances, it was more than could be expected.

Rank Insignia

Rank Badges

A far wider range of rank insignia was employed by the German Navy than any other branch of the German armed forces. These fell into three basic types: Seamen, Petty and Chief Petty Officers, Warrant Officers, and Commissioned Officers. German naval ranks were as follows:

Seamen and Petty Officers:

Matrose
Matrosen-Gefreiter
Matrosen-Obergefreiter
Matrosen-Hauptgefreiter
Matrosen-Stabsgefreiter
Matrosen-Stabsobergefreiter
Maat
Obermaat

Warrant Officers:

Bootsmann
Stabsbootsmann
Oberbootsmann
Stabsoberbootsmann

Commissioned Officers:

Fähnrich-zur-See
Oberfähnrich-zur-See
Leutnant-zur-See
Oberleutnant-zur-See
Korvettenkapitän
Fregattenkapitän
Kapitän-zur-See
Kommodore
Konteradmiral
Vizeadmiral
Admiral
Generaladmiral
Grossadmiral

Seamen, except cadets, wore chevrons as their badges of rank. These were worn on the upper left sleeve immediately above the elbow. These chevrons were often combined with trade insignia as one-piece badges. The chevrons were constructed in a V formed in a 60 degree angle, which had flat upper ends. The regulation length of the outer chevron was 8cm but could vary from 7cm to 8.3cm. When two or three chevrons were employed they were spaced 2-3mm apart. The chevron was placed onto a triangular patch, which was 1-3mm larger than the outer chevron and corresponded in colour to the garment onto which it was to be attached. Chevrons were in the form of gold-coloured tress (a long lock or ringlet) made of golden yellow badge cloth with cornflower blue trimming ribbon or of 1cm wide gold soutache braid with cornflower blue ribbon interwoven to form a 4mm wide chevron. Some ranks had a pip. This, in the same colour as the chevrons, was hand or machine-embroidered in gold, golden yellow or cornflower blue wool, cotton or artificial silk. It was centred between the chevrons, at a regulation distance of 2.7cm above the point of the chevron. Regulations required that the upper edge of the backing be horizontal. However, backings with a semi-circular top edge and combined with a career insignia are frequently encountered.

Rank insignia were not worn on boiler suits, leather jackets, U-boat tunics or brown tropical shirts, but for the other various garments were as follows:

Dress jackets and pea jackets: chevrons of gold tress or braided gold soutache (a narrow band used as a decorative trimming); pips of gold thread; backings of navy blue cloth. Seamen also wore plain cornflower blue-collar patches on pea jackets as a further indication of rank.

Blue shirts: chevrons cut out of golden yellow badge cloth in a width of 1cm or braided of 4mm wide stripes of golden yellow badge cloth or, rarely, gold soutache; pips of golden yellow wool, cotton or artificial silk; backing of navy blue cloth. The felt-like golden yellow cloth is encountered in various shades.

White shirts and working shirts: chevrons of cornflower blue trimming ribbon or braided 4mm wide cornflower blue ribbon; pips of cornflower blue cotton or artificial silk; backing of white fabric.

Field grey uniforms: chevrons of matt gold tress or braid of matt gold soutache; pip of golden yellow wool, cotton or artificial silk; backing of field grey or bluish dark green badge cloth or, during wartime, of field grey basic cloth. Chevrons on the off-white drill tunics of the Reichsmarine pattern were of cornflower blue trimming ribbon on a field of white drill fabric, while those of the field grey moleskin tunics were gold tress or gold soutache braid on a field of moleskin fabric.

Brown tropical uniforms: as for white shirts, but on a backing of tropical fabric. Chevrons of matt gold tress or soutache on a brown field were also used.

Photo 4 Boatswain Sea Services. Blue uniform.

Photo 5 Engine Room Personnel. Blue uniform. On ships with coal-fired boilers, the term was 'heizer' (stoker).

Career Insignia of Seamen

Seamen wore their career insignia on their upper left sleeves immediately above the rank chevrons, either as separate devices or in combination with the chevrons. If separate, the career symbol was embroidered on a 55mm round cloth base matching the uniform to which it was sewn. Insignia worn on blue or field grey uniforms were embroidered in yellow, and on white uniforms embroidered in cornflower blue. Some careers were not open to junior seamen grades but were open for petty officers only.

Boatswain – Sea Service

A five pointed star with a vertex of the star pointing upwards.

Engine Room Personnel

A cogwheel on a 55mm round cloth disc.

4

5

6

Signal Personnel

Two crossed signalling flags, bunting white with red border, on a 55mm round cloth disc.

Navigating Helmsman

Two crossed anchors, each positioned at a 45 degree angle, on a 55mm round cloth disc.

Helmsman/Coxswain

A sextant on a 55mm round cloth disc.

Telephone Operator

Three crossed lightning bolts superimposed on one another. Each end of the bolts has an arrowhead, on a 55mm round cloth disc. This was introduced on 1 October 1942.

Photo 6 Signal Personnel. Blue uniform. *Tim Stannard collection*

Photo 7 Navigating Helmsman. Blue uniform. Worn only by ratings after mid-1943 for MVBI No.453.

Photo 8 Helmsman/Coxswain. White uniform. *Tim Stannard collection*

Photo 9 Telephone Operator. Blue uniform. Introduced 1 October 1942 per MVBI No.891.

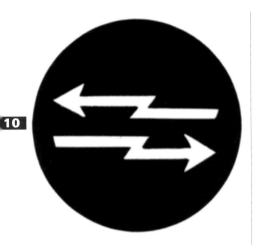

Radar Operator

Two horizontal lightning bolts, with their points in opposite directions, formed with a zigzag line and positioned one above the other on a 55mm round cloth disc. This was introduced on 15 January 1944.

Radio Operator

A lightning bolt pointing to the left and downwards on a 55mm round cloth disc.

Teletypist

Two crossed lightning bolts pointing downwards on a 55mm round cloth disc. Each bolt has two equidistant indentations, one above and the other below the line of the bolt.

Photo 10 Radar Operator. Blue uniform. Introduced 15 January 1944 per MVBI No.10.

Photo 11 Radio Operator. Blue uniform. *Tim Stannard collection*

Photo 12 Radio Operator. White uniform. *Tim Stannard collection*

Photo 13 Teletypist. Blue uniform. *Tim Stannard collection*

13

14

15

Carpenter

A pair of compasses with their points downwards on a 55mm round cloth disc.

Coastal Artillery

A winged flaming shell positioned vertically on a 55mm round cloth disc. This was introduced in 1935.

Administrative

A vertical staff of Mercury on a 55mm round cloth disc. This badge was introduced in 1935. The emblem was changed to a Latin letter V in about 1935 and to the Latin letter M (representing the Material administration) in about 1938.

Administrative

A Latin letter V on a 55mm round cloth disc. A badge featuring a staff of Mercury replaced this design in about 1935.

Material Administration Career

A Latin letter M on a 55mm round cloth disc. A badge featuring a staff of Mercury replaced this design in about 1936.

Photo 14 Coastal Artillery. Blue uniform. This was introduced in 1935. *Tim Stannard collection*

Photo 15 Administrative. Blue uniform. This was introduced in 1935. *Tim Stannard collection*

Photo 16 Carpenter. Blue uniform.

Photo 17 Administrative. White uniform.

Photo 18 Administrative. White uniform. Abolished after 1936; however still shown in 1938 uniform plates.

22

Motor Transport

A steering wheel with three spokes, one pointing upwards, on a 55mm round cloth disc. This was introduced on 31 July 1937.

Medical

A caduceus positioned vertically on a 55mm round cloth disc.

Blocking Weapons Mechanic

A mine with head upwards positioned vertically, superimposed on a cogwheel on a 55mm round cloth disc.

Photo 19 Motor Transport. Blue uniform. From 31 July 1937 per MVBI No.521. *Tim Stannard collection*

Photo 20 Motor Transport. White uniform. *Tim Stannard collection*

Photo 21 Blocking Weapon Mechanic. Blue uniform. This was worn vertically. *Tim Stannard collection*

Photo 22 Torpedo Mechanic. White uniform. *Tim Stannard collection*

Torpedo Mechanic

A horizontal torpedo head pointing to the left, superimposed on a cogwheel on a 55mm round cloth disc.

23

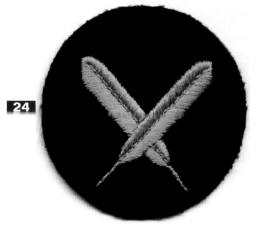

24

25

Telephone Mechanic

Three crossed lightning bolts superimposed on a cogwheel on a 55mm round cloth disc. Each end of the lightning bolts has an arrowhead that acts as a prolonged spoke.

Clerical

Two crossed feathers on a 55mm round cloth disc.

Musician

A vertically positioned lyre on a 55mm round cloth disc.

Photo 23 Telephone Mechanic. Blue uniform. Introduced by order MVBI No.432 on 1 July 1938. *Tim Stannard collection*

Photo 24 Clerical. Blue uniform. *Tim Stannard collection*

Photo 25 Clerical. White uniform. *Tim Stannard collection*

Aircraft Warning Service

A horizontal wing superimposed on two diagonal lightning bolts formed with a zigzag line, with arrowheads at each end, on a 55mm round cloth disc. This was introduced in 1938.

Photo 26 Musician. Blue uniform.

Photo 27 Aircraft Warning Service. Blue uniform. This badge was introduced in 1938. *Tim Stannard collection*

Anti-Aircraft

A flaming shell positioned vertically on a 55mm round cloth disc.

Photo 28 Ordnance/Artificer for Seamen. Blue uniform. This was for enlisted personnel only. Introduced on 1 February 1940 per MVBI No.28. *Tim Stannard collection*

Rank Insignia of Junior Non-Commissioned Officers

Photo 29 Artillery Mechanic. White uniform.
Tim Stannard collection

Ordnance/Artificer for Seamen

Two crossed muzzle-loading cannon barrels on a 55mm round cloth disc. This was introduced on 1 February 1940.

Artillery Mechanic

Two crossed muzzle-loading cannon barrels superimposed on a cogwheel, on a 55mm round cloth disc.

Petty and Chief Petty Officers

Petty officer grades displayed their rank by means of a sleeve insignia, which consisted of one or two clear or fouled anchors with the trade insignia superimposed on the anchor or crossing the anchor. These anchors were placed slightly above the centre of the insignia to allow for the addition of a chevron. Insignia were worn on the upper left sleeve. Flat woven gold braid was worn on the collar of the pea jacket and on the cuffs of the uniform jacket. The collar patches on the pea jacket had a single bar of silver cord for petty officers and two bars for chief petty officers. The silver colour was changed to gold on 1 December 1939.

Regulation size for the metal vertical anchor was 5.6cm long with 1-2mm flukes. The machine-embroidered form measured 4.8-6.2cm by 4.5-5cm, while the machine-embroidered form with crossed anchors measured about 3.8cm by 3.8cm. Metal chevrons of the Obermaat rank were formed at 90 degrees with an outward length of 3.2cm, width of 6mm and with a pearling design bordering the edge. Metal chevrons were attached to the backing by pins. Embroidered chevrons met at an angle of 85-110 degrees with a length of 2.6-3.3cm and a width of 4-8mm.

Dress jackets and pea jacket: the oval backing was of navy blue cloth with a regulation size of 9cm by 7cm. An underlay of a slightly convex oval metal plate usually stiffened the cloth field and had holes for the attachment of the pins of the insignia. Specimens of wartime production were frequently of grey zinc-based metal with a gold finish and four thin iron pins and an oval cardboard underlay substituting for the metal backing.

Blue shirt: anchor insignia and chevrons machine-embroidered in golden yellow wool, cotton or artificial silk. Field of navy blue cloth with dark blue fabric or black paper glued to the reverse.

White shirts, working shirts and working jackets: insignia and chevrons of cornflower blue machine embroidery; field of white drill or similar fabric, with thin white nettle fabric glued to the reverse and framed by a 3mm-wide linen ribbon. Regulation size was 10cm by 7.5cm.

Working jacket of boiler and engine personnel: insignia and chevron printed in blue on an oval white fabric field.

Field grey uniforms: petty officers wore shoulder straps similar to those worn by warrant officers on the blue uniform but slightly wider with gilt braid on a field grey base.

Warrant Officers' Rank and Career Badges

Warrant officers displayed their rank by means of shoulder straps. These straps were in dark blue cloth with flat gold braid edging and various combinations of aluminium pips to denote ranks. On the field grey uniform warrant officers wore shoulder straps similar to those worn on the blue uniform but slightly wider with gilt braid on a field grey base.

Boatswain

A fouled anchor.

Photo 31 Oberbootsmannsmaat. Metal version. Blue uniform. *Tim Stannard collection*

30

31

Photo 30 Boatswain. Bootsmannsmaat. Metal version. Blue uniform. *Tim Stannard collection*

32

34

Photo 32 Engineer.
Maschinenmaat. Metal version.
Blue uniform. *Tim Stannard
collection*

Photo 33 Engineer.
Obermaschinenmaat.
Metal version. Blue uniform.
Tim Stannard collection

Photo 34 Helmsman/
Coxswain. Steuermannsmaat.
Metal version. Blue uniform.
Tim Stannard collection

Photo 35 Navigating
Helmsman.
Vermessungssteuermannsmaat.
Metal version. Blue uniform.
Tim Stannard collection

Photo 36 Radio Operator.
Funkmaat. Metal version. Blue
uniform. *Tim Stannard collection*

Engineer

A cogwheel superimposed on an anchor.

Helmsman/Coxswain

Two crossed anchors, each positioned at a 45 degree angle to the vertical.

Navigating Helmsman

A sextant superimposed at the centre of crossed anchors.

Radio Operator

A lightning bolt pointing to the left and downwards, superimposed on an anchor.

Photo 37 Signaller. Signalmaat. Metal version. Blue uniform. *Tim Stannard collection*

Photo 38 Signaller. Obesignalmaat. Cloth form. Blue uniform. *Tim Stannard collection*

Photo 39 Teletypist. Fernschreibmaat. Metal version. Blue uniform. *Tim Stannard collection*

Photo 40 Telephone Mechanic. Fernsprechmechanikersmaat. Cloth version. White uniform.

Photo 41 Telephone Operator. Fernsprechmaat. Cloth version. Blue uniform.

Photo 42 Radar Operator. Funkmessdienst. Cloth version. Blue uniform.

Signaller

Two crossed signalling flags, in white bunting with a red border, superimposed on an anchor.

Telephone Mechanic

Three crossed lightning bolts superimposed on a cogwheel. Each end of the lightning bolts has an arrowhead that acts as a prolonged spoke. The whole emblem is superimposed on an anchor.

Teletypist

Two crossed lightning bolts pointing downwards, superimposed on an anchor. Each bolt has two equidistant indentations, one above and the other below the line of the bolt.

Telephone Operator

Three crossed lightning bolts superimposed on an anchor. Each end of the bolts has an arrowhead.

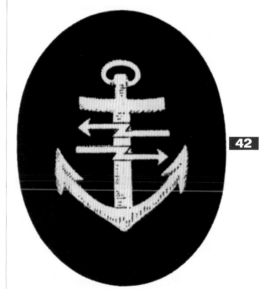

Radar Operator

Two horizontal lightning bolts formed with a zigzag line and positioned one above the other. They have their points in opposite directions and are superimposed on an anchor.

Photo 43 Carpenter. Zimmermannsmaat. Metal version. Blue uniform. *Tim Stannard collection*

Photo 44 Carpenter. Oberzimmermannsmaat. Metal version. Blue uniform. *Tim Stannard collection*

Carpenter

A pair of compasses with their points downwards, superimposed on an anchor.

Ordnance

Two crossed muzzle-loading cannon barrels superimposed on an anchor.

Artillery Mechanic

A cogwheel superimposed on two crossed muzzle-loading cannon barrels. The whole is then superimposed on an anchor.

Torpedo Mechanic

A horizontal torpedo head pointing to the left superimposed on a cogwheel. The whole is then superimposed on an anchor.

Photo 45 Ordnance. Oberfeberwerksmaat. Metal version. Blue uniform. *Tim Stannard collection*

Photo 45A Artillery Mechanics. Mechanikersmaat. Metal version. Blue uniform. *Tim Stannard collection*

Photo 46 Torpedo Mechanic. Torpedo Mechanikersmaat. Metal version. Blue uniform. *Tim Stannard collection*

Photo 47 Torpedo Mechanic. Torpedo Obermechaniksmaat. Metal version. Blue uniform. *Tim Stannard collection*

48

Blocking Weapons Mechanic

A mine with head upwards positioned at a 45 degree angle and superimposed on a cogwheel. The whole is then superimposed on an anchor, which is itself positioned at a 45 degree angle.

Photo 48 Blocking Weapons Mechanic. Sperrwaffen – Obermechanikersmaat. Metal version. Blue uniform. *Tim Stannard collection*

Photo 49 Administrator. Verwaltungsmaat. Metal version. Blue uniform. *Tim Stannard collection*

Photo 50 Clerk. Obers – Schreiberolermaat. Metal version. Blue uniform. *Tim Stannard collection*

Administrator

A vertical staff of Mercury superimposed on the haft of an anchor. This combination replaced the badge with a Latin letter V on the anchor and the Latin letter M on the anchor that applied to the material administrator career in about 1935.

Administrator

A Latin letter V superimposed on the haft of an anchor. The badge depicting a staff of Mercury replaced this design in about 1935.

28

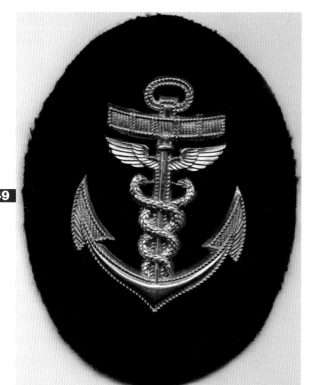

Material Administrator

A Latin letter M superimposed on the haft of an anchor. The badge depicting a staff of Mercury replaced this design in about 1935.

Clerk

Two crossed feathers superimposed on an anchor.

Medical Branch

A caduceus positioned at a 45 degree angle and superimposed on an anchor, which is itself positioned at a 45 degree angle.

Photo 51 Medical Branch. Sanitätemaat. Metal version. Blue uniform. *Tim Stannard collection*

52

53

54

Musician

A vertically positioned lyre superimposed on the haft of an anchor.

Coastal Artillery

A winged flaming shell positioned vertically and superimposed on the haft of an anchor.

Motor Transport

A steering wheel with three spokes, one pointing upwards, superimposed on the haft of an anchor.

Replacement Service

A plain anchor positioned vertically. This was introduced on 15 September 1937.

Aircraft Warning Service

A horizontal wing superimposed on two diagonal lightning bolts formed with a zigzag line, with arrowheads at each end. The whole is then superimposed on an anchor

Photo 52 Musician. Musikmaat. Metal version. Blue uniform. *Tim Stannard collection*

Photo 53 Coastal Artillery. Marineartilleriemaat. Metal version. Blue uniform. *Tim Stannard collection*

Photo 54 Coastal Artillery. Marineartillerieobermaat. Metal version. Blue uniform. *Tim Stannard collection*

Photo 55 Motor Transport. Kraftfahrmaat. Metal version. Blue uniform. *Tim Stannard collection*

Photo 56 Aircraft Warning Service. Flugmeldemaat. Cloth version. Blue uniform. *Tim Stannard collection*

Career Insignia for Cadets

Sea Cadet

A five-pointed star with a vertex of the star pointing upwards. This is placed on an oval cloth disc with a border of four lines of stitching.

Defensive Ordnance Cadet

A mine with head upwards positioned vertically on an oval cloth disc which has a border of four lines of stitching.

Naval Medical Cadet

A caduceus positioned vertically and placed on an oval cloth disc with a border of four lines of stitching.

Photo 57 Sea Cadet. Seekadetten. Blue uniform. *Tim Stannard collection*

Photo 58 Defensive Ordnance Cadet. Kadetten des Sperrwaffenwesens. Blue uniform.

Photo 59 Naval Medical Cadet. Marinesanitätskadetten. Blue uniform.

Naval Engineer Cadet

A cogwheel on an oval cloth disc with a border of four lines of stitching.

Technical Communications Cadet

A cogwheel superimposed over a lightning bolt pointing to the left and downwards, on an oval cloth disc with a border of four lines of stitching.

Communications Cadet

A lightning bolt pointing to the left and downwards, on an oval cloth disc with a border of four lines of stitching.

Photo 60 Naval Engineer Cadet. Kadetten des Marine – Ingenieurwesens. Blue uniform.

Photo 61 Technical Communications Cadet. Kadetten des technischen Nachrichtenwesens. Blue uniform.

Photo 62 Communications Cadet. Kadetten des Marinenachrichtenwesens. Blue uniform.

Marine Artillery Cadet

A winged flaming shell, positioned vertically, on an oval cloth disc with a border of four lines of stitching.

Ordnance Cadet

Two crossed cannon, on an oval cloth disc with a border of four lines of stitching.

Administration Cadet

Staff of Mercury, on an oval cloth disc with a border of four lines of stitching.

Cadet, Official's Career

A national military eagle holding a swastika, on an oval cloth disc with a border of four lines of stitching.

Photo 63 Marine Artillery Cadet. Marineartilleriekadetten. Blue uniform.

Photo 64 Cadet, Officer's Career. Marinebaubeamtenkadetten. Insigne for the left sleeve. The insigne for the right sleeve had the eagle head facing in the opposite direction. Blue uniform. *Tim Stannard collection*

63

Commissioned Officers' Rank Badges

64

To denote specific ranks the blue uniform had a system of rings on the jacket sleeves. These were constructed from flat woven gilt braid. This was complemented by braid on the peak of the cap. The cap peak was covered in blue cloth on which was embroidered in gilt wire a pattern of oak leaves. On the white summer uniform and greatcoat the sleeve rings were not employed. Towards the end of the war sleeve rings were not worn on the reefer jacket either.

Shoulder straps were made from matt silver braid on a dark blue cloth base, which were modelled on the Army pattern. Admirals had triple cord, the outer cords in silver with the centre one in gilt. To denote individual ranks aluminium pips were employed. Only the highest rank of Grand Admiral had crossed admiral's batons. On the field grey uniform, shoulder straps followed the same pattern as the blue uniform, but the base colour was dark green. Officers from Leutnant to Kommodore wore silver wire-embroidered collar patches with two yellow strips. Admirals wore collar tabs embroidered in gold wire based on the design for Army generals but with a blue background instead of red.

Career Insignia of Officers

The insignia of the respective branches of the service were worn on the lower right and left sleeves positioned above the rank stripes. The career sleeve insignia were either hand-embroidered in gold wire or machine-embroidered in yellow thread on an oval of navy blue badge cloth. Where appropriate the heads of insignia always faced forwards; for example, the head of the snake in the symbol for the medical career faced to the wearer's front.

The insignia were worn on the sleeves of the reefer jacket, frock coat and the blue mess jacket.

Engineer Officer

A cogwheel on an oval cloth disc.

Administrative Officer

Staff of Mercury on an oval cloth disc.

Photo 65 Engineer Officer. Oberleutnant. Blue uniform. *Tim Stannard collection*

Photo 66 Administrative Officer. Verwaltungsoffizier. Blue uniform. *Tim Stannard collection*

67

Officer Administrative Branch of the Truppensonderdienst

Staff of Mercury with a bar beneath, on an oval cloth disc The bar denotes the Truppensonderdienst (TSD).

Blocking Weapons Ordnance Officer

A mine with head upwards positioned verti-cally on an oval cloth disc.

Medical Officer

A caduceus positioned vertically on an oval cloth disc.

Photo 67 Officer Administrative Branch of the Truppensonderdienst. The bar below denoted the TSB and not 'called up from reserve status' as occasionally attributed. *Tim Stannard collection*

Photo 68 Blocking Weapons Ordnance Officer. Waffenoffizier (Sperrwaffen). Blue uniform. *Tim Stannard collection*

Photo 69 Medical Officer. Sanitätsoffizier. Blue uniform. *Tim Stannard collection*

Photo 70 Line Officer. Seeoffizier. Blue uniform. *Tim Stannard collection*

Photo 71 Line Officer (reserve). Blue uniform.

36

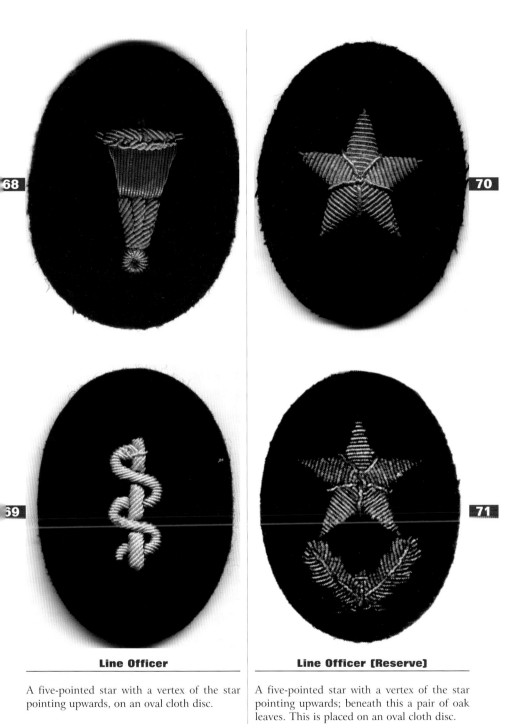

68

70

69

71

Line Officer	Line Officer [Reserve]
A five-pointed star with a vertex of the star pointing upwards, on an oval cloth disc.	A five-pointed star with a vertex of the star pointing upwards; beneath this a pair of oak leaves. This is placed on an oval cloth disc.

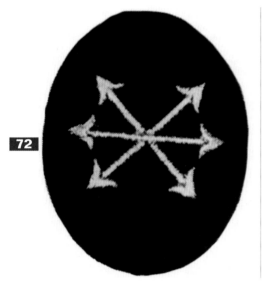

Photo 72 Telephone Operator Officer. Blue uniform.

Photo 73 Communications Officer. Marinenachrichtenoffizier. Blue uniform. The insignia was for the right sleeve.

Photo 74 Technical Communications Officer. Technische – Nachrichtenoffizier. Blue uniform. The insignia was for the right sleeve. *Tim Stannard collection*

Photo 75 Coastal Artillery Officer. Marineartillerie. Blue uniform.

Photo 76 Ordnance Officer. Waffenoffizier. Blue uniform. *Tim Stannard collection*

Photo 77 Midshipman of the officials' career. The insigne depicts that worn on the left sleeve of the blue uniform. Candidates of certain branches of officials were trained together with the officer candidates, and rank among these with the status of soldiers.
When the officer candidates were eventually promoted to Leutnant, the officer candidates of officials career were promoted to the appropriate official rank. *Tim Stannard collection*

Communications Officer

A lightning bolt pointing to the left and downwards, on an oval cloth disc.

Technical Communications Officer

A lightning bolt pointing to the left and downwards with at the centre a rosette. This is placed on an oval cloth disc.

Coastal Artillery Officer

A winged flaming shell, positioned vertically, on an oval cloth disc.

Midshipman of the Official's Career

A national military eagle holding a swastika, on an oval cloth disc. Candidates for the officials' branch were trained together with the officer candidates.

Ordnance Officer

Crossed muzzle-loading cannons on an oval cloth disc.

Telephone Operator Officer

Three crossed lightning bolts. Each end of the bolts has an arrowhead. This is placed on an oval cloth disc. Introduced by Order MV42, No 891 on 22 October 1942.

Duty Badges

Officer of the Watch

An oval gold pressed-metal badge featuring an oak-leaf wreath surrounding a fouled anchor. The reverse was hollow pressed and had a pin attachment, spring clip or two loops and a cotter-key type pin. The regulation size was 6.4cm by 5.2cm, but in some cases this varied. The badge was worn by officers of the watch on ships or the duty officer of land units. It was for identification rather than qualification, the badge marking a position of responsibility. The badge was not the property of the individual and was removed when the watch tour was completed and passed from the watch officer to his relief. It was worn on the left breast pocket whether in the metal form or in the cloth version (usually affixed by snaps to the uniform). It could also be worn on the upper left sleeve as a 9cm-wide armband made

Photo 78 Naval officer wearing the Officer of the Watch badge.

Photo 79 Duty badge for Officer of the Watch. This is a pressed metal badge which is gilded. *Tim Stannard collection*

Photo 80 Reverse of the badge showing the spring clip. *Tim Stannard collection*

of white cloth or glossy white leather. The armband had the badge attached to its centre. The leather armband was lined with white cotton cloth.

The watch badge was worn in the following manner on other uniforms.

Greatcoat: clasped into the second button-hole from above.

Frock coat: from the buttonhole of the left lapel.

Reefer jacket: attached above the slit of the left breast pocket or above the uppermost button of the left row of buttons.

With the four-pocket jacket of any kind including the brown tropical tunic: from the buttonhole of the left breast pocket. The badge was possibly worn with the *field grey uniform* but this was not mentioned in regulations.

81

Photo 81 Badge of Staff Personnel. Blue uniform.

Badge of Staff Personnel

The insignia was a machine-embroidered admiral's flag, the design being a white flag measuring 2cm square decorated with a black Iron Cross bordered by a black and white outer line and with a yellow pole extending 2mm above and 5mm below at the left edge. This was executed on a 6cm diameter circular patch. The embroidery was of wool on a navy backing for blue garments. For white garments the embroidery was in cotton or artificial silk threads on a backing of blue nankeen with blue nettle glued to the reverse. There was a narrow blue linen ribbon border around the edge.

NCOs and seamen on the staffs of sea (fleet) commanders were identified by the insignia, which was introduced by order MV 37, No 347, dated 18 June 1937. The badge was also required to be worn by junior NCOs and seamen on the staff of flotilla leaders. Junior NCOs and seamen wore the badge on the left sleeve of all blue and white garments above all other rank, career or specialist insignia. Senior NCOs wore the badge on the upper left sleeve of reefer jackets and white jackets only, with further wear being discontinued by order MV 36, No 482, dated 25 August 1936. This was the only insignia that was worn on the white garments that had a blue backing.

Insignia of Aviso 'Grille'

This badge has an insignia depicting the *Führerstandarte*. This is in the form of a square of red material, with a white disc in the centre. Set just inside this disc is a circular garland of gold-coloured oak leaves decorated in four equidistant places, top, bottom, left and right with a wide band of gold-coloured ribbon. Set on the white disc inside the garland is a black upright swastika. Edged with a black and white border, the arms of the swastika extend to the inner edge of the garland of oak leaves. In each corner of the red field is an eagle emblem. Appearing in the upper left corner and lower right corner are gold-coloured party eagles and swastikas and in the other two opposite corners are gold-coloured Wehrmacht eagles. The swastikas on these emblems are positioned nearest to the corners and the heads of all four eagles face in an anti-clockwise direction. The entire standard is edged on all four sides with a double border with a wide outer band of black and narrow inner band of white. This whole item was produced in screen-printed cloth centred on a white armband. It is presumed that it was

Photo 82
Armbands of the
Aviso 'Grille' and
the OKW in wear.

82

issued to members of the crew of the motor-boat that ferried Hitler to his yacht or by Hitler's personal orderly of the day. It was worn on the upper right sleeve.

Insignia for Escort of Oberkommando der Wehrmacht

An insignia depicting the flag of the Oberkommando der Wehrmacht, which consisted of a white square with a thin line border indented from the broader outer border. At the centre of the white field produced is a square flag, broken by horizontal bars of, from the top, black, white and red. Superimposed on these is an Iron Cross. In each quarter, heads facing to the Iron Cross is a Wehrmacht eagle with a swastika in its talons. The whole item was produced in screen-printed cloth centred on a white armband. The flag for the Minister of War and Oberkommando der Wehrmacht ceased to be used after 4 February 1938 and in its place the *Führerstandarte* was employed. This helps date the period of use of the armband.

Sleeve Badges of Specialists

Junior NCOs and seamen who had successfully completed training in a special function were permitted to wear a badge that denoted this achievement. The specialist badges worn on blue garments were machine-embroidered in red cotton or artificial silk thread on an oval underlay measuring 9cm in height and 7cm in width with glued on blue nettle on the reverse. Badges worn on white shirts and white work shirts were embroidered in red cotton or matt or glossy artificial silk thread on an underlay of white cotton drill or similar cloth, with white nettle glued to the reverse and bordered by a white 4-5.5cm wide linen ribbon. The embroidery was on the centre axis and of a size that did not touch the border of the underlay. If there were chevrons below the insignia, the insignia was off-centre and frequently also slightly smaller than without the chevrons. Wartime production badges were frequently without the glued on nettle on the reverse or without the linen ribbon around the badge. A few selected badges were permitted for wear with the field grey Navy uniform until 1933. In later years, and against regulations, the badges were still sometimes worn with the field grey uniform. These badges had a field grey backing.

One or more specialist badges could be worn together on the left sleeve of all blue uniform garments, worn below all career and rank insignia. Junior officer candidates and cadets did not wear any specialist badges. However, order MV 44, No 110, dated 25 February 1944, permitted wear of the badges after promotion to cadet, provided they had been previously acquired. They were removed on promotion to junior officer candidate.

The following range of badges was in use for some or most of the period 1933-40.

1. **Gunner of Automatic Anti-Aircraft Weapons**
Flaming shell. This was abolished around 1938 and Badge 2 renamed as a gunner or observer's award. By order OTB 39, No 107 IV, dated 7 May 1939 as Flak S.

2. **Observer of Automatic Anti-Aircraft Weapons**
Flaming winged shell. By order OTB 39, No 107 IV, dated 7 May 1939 as Flak B.

3. **Gun Chief 2nd Class**
Flaming shell with one chevron. By order MV 36, No 342, dated 13 June 1936, it was renamed G.F.E.

Photo 83 Gun Chief 2nd Class. Blue uniform. *Tim Stannard collection*

4. Gun Chief 1st Class
Flaming shell with two chevrons. By order MV 36, No 342, dated 13 June 1936, it was renamed G.F.T.

5. Gun Chief E
Flaming shell with one chevron with a non-embroidered letter E on the shell. By order MV 36, No 342, dated 13 June 1936, it was renamed G.F.E.

5a. Gun Chief E (after three years as such)
Flaming shell with two chevrons with a non-embroidered letter E on the shell.

5b. Gun Chief E (after six years as such)
Flaming shell with three chevrons with a non-embroidered letter E on the shell.

Photo 84 Gun Chief. 1st Class. Blue uniform. *Tim Stannard collection*

Photo 85 Gun Chief of Heavy Artillery of Ships. White Uniform. *Tim Stannard collection*

Photo 86 Auxiliary Torpedo Instructor. Blue uniform. *Tim Stannard collection*

6. Gun Chief T
Flaming shell with one chevron with a non-embroidered letter T on the shell.

6a. Gun Chief T (after three years as such)
Flaming shell with two chevrons with a non-embroidered letter T on the shell.

6b. Gun Chief T (after six years as such)
Flaming shell with three chevrons with a non-embroidered letter T on the shell.

7. Gun Chief R
Flaming shell with two crossed oak leaves below. Introduced by order MV 36, No 342, dated 13 June 1936.

8. Gun Chief of AA Gun
Flaming winged shell. This was renamed by order OTB 20, No 107 IV, dated 7 May 1939 as G.F.Flak I.

9. Gun Chief of Heavy Artillery of Ships
Flaming shell with three chevrons.

10. Artillery Control Foreman
Two dials pointing to each other, on a disc with a graduated border, with a black-bordered letter A in the centre.

11. Torpedo Control Foreman
Two dials pointing to each other, on a disc with a graduated border, with a black-bordered letter T in the centre.

11a. Torpedo Control Foreman Grade III
Two dials pointing to each other, on a disc with a graduated border, with a black-bordered letter T in the centre, with one chevron. Introduced by order MV 36, No 730, dated 10 December 1936, to replace badge 11.

11b. Torpedo Control Foreman Grade II
Two dials pointing to each other, on a disc with a graduated border, with a black-bordered letter T in the centre, with two chevrons. Introduced by order MV 36, No 730, dated 10 December 1936, as a sub-division of badge 11 torpedo control foreman, which was renumbered 11a.

11c. Torpedo Control Foreman Grade I
Two dials pointing to each other, on a disc with a graduated border, with a black-bordered letter T in the centre, with three chevrons. Introduced by order MV 36, No 730, dated 10 December 1936.

12. AA Weapons Control Foreman
Two dials pointing to each other, on a disc with a graduated border, with a black-bordered letter F in the centre.

13. Coastal Guns Control Foreman
Two dials pointing to each other, on a disc with a graduated border, with a black-bordered letter K in the centre.

14. Rangefinder Operator
Rangefinder on top of an equilateral triangle, with a small flaming shell within the triangle.

15. Rangefinder Operator, AA Guns
Rangefinder on top of an equilateral triangle, with wings at the side of the triangle with a small flaming shell within the triangle.

16. Torpedo Gunner
Torpedo with one chevron.

17. Auxiliary Torpedo Instructor
Torpedo with two chevrons.

18. Blockade Weapons Foreman
Mine.

19. Blockade Weapons Foreman
Mine with two crossed oak leaves. Introduced by order MV 36, No 342, dated 13 June 1936.

20. Member of Drum and Fife Corps
Two chevrons at a 90 degree angle, pointing upwards, the upper chevron with an oval loop at the point.

21. Surveying Service
Latin letter V. Abolished by order MV 40, No 2, dated 23 December 1939, after constitution of surveying career.

22. Ship Diver
Diver's helmet with three blue windows.

23. Torpedo Diver
Diver's helmet with three blue windows, with one chevron.

24. Sports Instructor

Gothic letters Lb. This was replaced by the Gothic letters Sp by order MV 34, No 62, dated 10 February 1935. Lb was the abbreviation for *Leibesubungen* or body exercise.

24a. Sports Instructor

Gothic letters Sb. This was introduced by order MV 34, No 62, dated 10 February 1935. Sb was the abbreviation for *Sport* (same word in German).

25a. Specialist in Electric Motors with E. III – Course

Cogwheel seen from left front, with four lightning bolts out of either hub.

25b. Specialist in Electric Motors with E. II – Course

Cogwheel seen from left front, with four lightning bolts out of either hub, with one chevron.

25c. Specialist in Electric Motors with E. I – Course

Cogwheel seen from left front, with four lightning bolts out of either hub, with two chevrons.

26a. Motor Specialist with Mot. III – Course

Propeller with three blades with one blade pointing upwards.

26b. Motor Specialist with Mot. II – Course

Propeller with three blades with one blade pointing upwards, with one chevron.

26c. Motor Specialist with Mot. I – Course

Propeller with three blades with one blade pointing upwards, with two chevrons.

27. Hydrophone Operator

Downward-pointing arrow passing through four wave lines. This was introduced by order MV 35, No 401, dated 30 October 1935.

28. AA Sound Locator Operator

Upward-pointing arrow passing through two curved lines. This was introduced by order MV 36, No. 490, dated 31 August 1936.

29. AA Searchlight Controller

Upward-pointed arrow passing through two curved lines with one chevron. This was introduced by order MV 37, No. 314, dated 4 June 1937.

30. Motor Driver

Cogwheel with canted red black-bordered letter K. This was abolished by order MV 36, No 503, dated 5 September 1936, after constitution of the driver's career.

31. Teletype Operator

Two crossed lightning bolts pointing downwards. This was abolished by order MV 34, No 34, dated 16 January 1934, after constitution of the teletype operator career.

On 9 August 1940 a new list of specialist badges was published. Some badges were renamed or their design changed. Badges No 4, 5, 6, 20, 21 and 22 were renamed by order MV 40, No 685, dated 16 September 1940. Those not listed anymore were abolished.

1. Gun Chief of Smaller Vessels

Unchanged.

2. Gun Chief of Medium Artillery of Ships

Unchanged.

3. Gun Chief of Heavy Artillery

Unchanged.

4. Gunner and Observer of Automatic AA Weapons

Unchanged.

5. Gun Chief of Light AA Guns

Unchanged.

6. Gun Chief of Heavy AA Guns

Unchanged.

7. Rangefinder Operator

Unchanged.

8. Rangefinder Operator (Careers I and XIV)

Rangefinder on top of a unilateral triangle, with one chevron.

Photo 87 AA Searchlight Controller. Blue uniform. *Tim Stannard collection*

9. Rangefinder Operator with Training as Petty Officer
Rangefinder on top of a unilateral triangle, with two chevrons.

10. Weapons Control Foreman (Unit Trained)
Two dials pointing to each other on a disc with a graduated border.

11. Weapons Control Foreman Artillery, AA Guns, and Coastal Guns
Two dials pointing to each other on a disc with a graduated border, with one chevron.

12. Torpedo Control Foreman Grade III
Unchanged.

13. Torpedo Control Foreman Grade II
Unchanged.

14. Blockade Weapons Foreman
Mine with one chevron.

15. Ship Diver
Unchanged.

16. Torpedo Diver
Diver's helmet with two chevrons.

17. U-boat and Salvage Diver
Diver's helmet with three chevrons.

18. Seaman Hydrophone Operator
Arrow pointing downwards, with one chevron.

19. Hydrophone Petty Officers
Arrow pointing downwards, with two chevrons.

20. AA Sound Locator (Unit Trained)
Upward-pointing arrow. After necessary alterations.

21. AA Sound Locator
Upward-pointing arrow, with one chevron.

22. AA Searchlight Controller
Upward-pointing arrow, with two chevrons.

23. Technical Searchlight Course Coast
Unchanged.

24. Electric Techniques Grade III
Cogwheel seen from left with four lightning bolts out of either hub, with one chevron.

25. Electric Techniques Grade II
Cogwheel seen from left with four lightning bolts out of either hub, with two chevrons.

26. Motor Course Grade III
Unchanged.

27. Motor Course Grade II
Propeller with three blades (one pointing upwards), with two chevrons.

28. Member of Drum and Fife Corps
Unchanged.

29. Gun Chief of Coastal Guns (Unit Trained)
Flaming bomb.

30. Gun Chief of Coastal Guns
Flaming bomb, with two chevrons.

31. Gun Chief of AA Guns (Unit Trained)
Winged flaming bomb.

There were further revisions on 18 June 1941.

14a. Blocking Weapons Specialist
Mine with one chevron.

14b. Blocking Weapons Foreman
Mine with two chevrons.

There was a final change on 23 February 1942.

Mine Foreman
Mine foremen were given the same badge (mine with one chevron) as blocking weapons specialists.

Photo 88 Electric Techniques Grade II. Blue uniform. *Tim Stannard collection*

Photo 89 Electric Techniques Grade II. White uniform. *Tim Stannard collection*

48

Spanish Civil War Awards

On 17 July 1936 a revolt against the Spanish Republic broke out in many of the military garrisons in Spanish Morocco. The revolt was led by Generals Mola and Franco, the latter having been the governor of the Canary Islands until his dismissal by the Popular Front government. The rising spread rapidly throughout Spain, resulting in serious fighting between government troops and anti-government forces.

For several years Spanish generals and other agents had been in contact with, and successfully seeking support from, both Hitler and Mussolini. Hitler, who was wholly committed to oppose what he saw as the Communist threat in western Europe, made the decision within a few days of the Nationalist rebellion to stand by Franco and actively to support him in his 'fight against Bolshevism'.

On 31 July 1936 the first detachment of eighty-five German air and ground crew 'volunteers', travelling as a party of tourists, left Hamburg for Cadiz on the Woermann liner *Usamoro*. They took with them six Heinkel 51 fighters. Simultaneously twenty Junkers 52 transport planes piloted by German airmen were flown from Berlin to Morocco. It had been recognised that the most valuable service Germany could render Franco at this stage was to help him ferry his Moorish troops into Spain.

Under the command of Hauptmann Henke, forty-two Luftwaffe pilots began to ferry Franco's Moroccan troops of the Spanish Foreign Legion from Tetuán to the aerodrome of Tablada at Seville. The first flights were made with twenty-two soldiers and their equipment on board each plane. On later flights the number of passengers carried on each plane was increased to thirty. Untiring,

sometimes four or five times a day, Henke and his pilots flew to and fro. By the beginning of September this small unit had transported from Africa to the Spanish mainland the astonishing number, for its time, of 8,899 soldiers, along with forty-four field guns, ninety machine guns and 137 tons of ammunition and equipment.

At the onset of the uprising, most of the Spanish Navy had remained loyal to the government, though many officers had been executed for disloyalty. When Franco had initially requested German assistance he received, beside the air and ground support, a small naval contingent. This small unit numbered only three officers and about ten specialists in coastal artillery, mine warfare and radio communications. These first German naval volunteers found that the only vessels in Nationalist hands were the cruiser *Almirante Cervera* the destroyer *Belasco*, the liner *España*, and several small gunboats, all without trained officers.

From July 1936 the Kriegsmarine also sent warships to Spain with the dual mission of evacuating German nationals caught up in the conflagration, and protecting German merchant shipping in Spanish waters (other navies also sent warships to Spain with similar missions). The German submarines *U-33* and *U-34* were already on station in Spanish waters and the pocket battleship *Deutschland* appeared off Ceuta. The *Deutschland* and the *Admiral Scheer* were to remain in Spanish waters for most of the war, with one or the other being occasionally relieved by the *Admiral Graf Spee*. They were normally supported by four of Germany's six cruisers, one torpedo boat flotilla and several submarines.

In September 1936, Oberstleutnant Walter Warlimont, a general staff officer from the Army High Command, was appointed Plenipotentiary Delegate of the Wehrmacht in Spain. Admiral Rolf Carls was appointed the German Naval Commander in Spanish waters. In October 1936 he outlined for his commanders the objectives of the Kriegsmarine in Spain as:

1. Protection and escort of the special steamers engaged in the covert, priority trade with Insurgent ports.

2. Protection of German interests and German citizens.

3. Reconnaissance on behalf of the insurgents and transmission of intelligence thus gained to 'Guido' [Warlimont] at Franco's headquarters in Salamanca, later Burgos.

4. Reconnaissance for the purpose of gathering evidence about Russian shipments of war material to the Republic, for submission by the German Foreign Office to the Non-Intervention Committee in London.

To exercise administrative supervision over the entire Spanish operation, Special Staff 'W' was formed. A unit known as the 'Shipping Department' was created within the special staff by the Navy and tasked with organising and controlling every aspect of Germany's maritime arms traffic with Franco's Spain.

Foreign interventions have an inherent tendency to spiral upwards and sometimes get out of control. Spain was to be no exception. Within six months of its arrival in Spanish waters, the Kriegsmarine was in practice waging an indirect and undeclared war against the Spanish Republic. Realising that the Spanish Civil War was likely to last a long time, Hitler decided in November 1936 to increase Germany's economic and military commitment. With the resulting deployment of the Legion Condor a new and larger naval contingent arrived in Spain under the codename Gruppe Nordsee. The group staff shared the facilities of the German naval attaché, while instructors were billeted in Cadiz and Palma de Mallorca. The group was under the command of Korvettenkapitän Hans Schottky and its mission was to train the Spaniards in ship and coastal gunnery, mine warfare, communications and in torpedo boat warfare. There was also a Kriegsmarine Sea Transport Group in Vigo assigned to distributing supplies to the Legion.

Despite the setting up of a European non-intervention committee, of which Germany was a member, intended to prevent interna-tional participation in the Spanish Civil War, Germany thus, very swiftly, and secretly, set about organising a powerful, semi-autonomous air component for collaboration with General Franco. An example of the lengths to which the German government was prepared to go in order to deny to the world the existence of the Legion and the commitment of arms and men to Franco can be seen from the decree published in Germany on 20 February 1937. This forbade German nationals to enter Spain or Spanish possessions, including Spanish Morocco, in order to take part in the Civil War. The decree further empowered the Minister of the Interior, Hans Frick, to take the necessary measures to prevent the departure from, or transit through, Germany of volunteers, German or foreign. It should be noted that this decree was promulgated over three months after the formation of the Legion Condor.

Besides training Spanish naval personnel throughout the war, the Navy also established and operated an officer's training school at San Fernando. Twelve petty officers under the command of Kapitänleutnant Rolf Rüggeberg arrived and joined, as instructors, the 'Imker' organisation. They stayed on until the end of the war in 1939, but Rüggeberg remained in Spain until June 1940 as chief instructor at the school.

During the years of the Spanish Civil War, most operational German naval ships were given an opportunity to take part in the action. Like the Luftwaffe and Army, the German Navy used the war in Spain as a training ground.

On 14 April 1939, after the end of the war had been proclaimed, Hitler announced the institution of an award for bravery for the members of the Condor Legion, which was also to serve as a campaign medal: this was the Spanish Cross of the Legion Condor.

On 12 May, before they left Spain, General Franco decorated fifteen German (and eight Italian) flyers with Spain's second highest military decoration, the Military Medal. The victory parade celebrating the Nationalist triumph in the Civil War was held in Madrid on 19 May 1939. Over 42,000 troops representing all units of the Nationalist forces marched past including 3,500 men of the

German Legion Condor under Generalmajor von Richthofen, who brought up the rear of the parade.

A final farewell parade was held for the Legion at León in northwest Spain on 23 May 1939. Generalmajor von Richthofen presented his troops with Spanish decorations of varying grades in the name of Generalissimo Franco. Two days later the German troops began to embark on six 'Strength through Joy' ships that had arrived at Vigo and shortly afterwards set sail for Germany. Before leaving Spain the German and the Italian Legionaries handed over their arms and war materials to the Spanish government.

The Legion Condor landed at Hamburg on 30 May 1939 and received an official welcome from General Feld Marschall Göring. Göring announced that Hitler had instituted a new decoration, the Spanish Cross, in four classes of Bronze, Silver, Gold and Gold with Brilliants. All 'volunteers' who had served during the Civil War were to receive one of the four classes. It was further announced that the Legion Condor was to be officially dissolved within a few days and that in proud memory of the Legion the name 'Condor' had been bestowed by Hitler on a Luftwaffe wing: an anti-aircraft regiment and a signals battalion. A few days after their arrival in Hamburg the troops of the Legion proceeded to Döberitz, the military centre near Berlin. Here on 4 June Grossadmiral Raeder, the Commander-in-Chief of the German Navy, visited them. Raeder distributed decorations to the naval contingent and Göring presented decorations to Luftwaffe members of the Legion.

On 6 June 1939 Berlin was the venue for a special ceremony held in the Marble Gallery of the new Reich Chancellery. Here Hitler, accompanied by Göring, presented the Spanish Cross in Gold to Luftwaffe officers of the Legion Condor and Kriegsmarine officers from the pocket battleship *Deutschland*. It would appear that there was no specific regulation governing the grade of award given; generally the grade of the cross tended to be related to the rank of recipient, though it also seems to have been dependent upon the highest Spanish decoration the German serviceman had received.

Recipients of the Campaign Medal were awarded the Spanish Cross in Bronze with Swords.

Recipients of the Red Military Service Cross received the Spanish Cross in Silver with Swords.

Recipients of the Military Medal of the Breast Star to the War Cross were awarded the Spanish Cross in Gold with Swords.

The criteria for the award were one or more of:

1. To have been a volunteer in the Condor Legion and to have fought in Spain.

2. To have taken part in selected naval actions:

   a) The air attack on 29 May 1937 on the *Deutschland* in the waters off Ibiza.

   b) The bombing on 31 May of Almería in reprisal for the attack on the *Deutschland*.

3. Three months' continuous service in Spanish waters.

4. Performance of special acts of valour or merit, in a combat situation.

The Spanish Cross without Swords was rendered to non-combatant military personnel serving in Spain or Spanish Morocco. It could also be awarded to civilians and technicians who had taken part in assisting the forces in Spain. This was to include employees of Lufthansa who ferried materials and aircraft to Spain. This probably accounts for the relative rarity of the bronze and silver crosses and the fact that no gold crosses were awarded.

The grade awarded was dependent upon the highest Spanish decoration a German volunteer received.

Civilians and non-combatants who received the Campaign Medal were awarded the Spanish Cross in Bronze without Swords.

Civilians and non-combatants who received the Red Military Service Cross were awarded the Spanish Cross in Silver without Swords.

The criteria for the award were:

1. Three months' service in Spain.

2. An act that substantially assisted the war effort but not in a combat situation.

Regulations dated 10 August 1939 prescribed conditions for award and wear and stipulated that recommendations for awards must come from the Armed Forces High Command over the signature of the office of the Führer.

One particularly notable incident during the war was a Republican attack on the *Deutschland*. The Nazis regarded this as an outrage and Hitler made sure that the incident received renewed publicity when the awards of the cross were rendered. The *Deutschland* was attacked in Ibiza harbour by two Soviet pilots who thought they were bombing Franco's flagship, the *Canarias*. After the attack the *Deutschland* sailed to Gibraltar where it disembarked the dead and wounded, who were cared for at a British military hospital. This led to a number of awards to British medical personnel of the German Red Cross Decoration 1937-9 in varying grades. Funerals were conducted in Gibraltar, but the dead were later disinterred and returned to Germany on board the *Deutschland*, and given a state funeral on 17 June 1937. The final death toll was 32 with 73 wounded.

Known British recipients of the German Red Cross Decoration were one matron, twelve sisters and other medical staff at the military hospital at Gibraltar and these included:

Captain John Primrose Douglas RAMC, Cross of Merit, 26 July 1937

Sister Catherine McShane, Frauenkreuz, 26 July 1937

Mrs M.G. Burton, Frauenkreuz, 26 July 1937

Mrs Margaret Paula Lewis, Frauenkreuz, 26 July 1937

Miss Cargill Lockhead, Frauenkreuz, 26 July 1937

Miss Nora Smyth, Frauenkreuz, 26 July 1937

Commander H.J. Murphy, Cross of Merit, 13 January 1938

Nora Smyth ended her service as a lieutenant-colonel in the British Army nursing service. Her British medals were Royal Red Cross 1st Class, 1939-1945 Star, Africa Star, Italy Star, Defence Medal and War Medal.

Spanish Cross with Swords – Bronze, Silver and Gold Classes

Instituted: 14 April 1939
Number awarded: 8,462; 8,304; 1,126
Rarity: scarce, scarce, rare

Known maker(s)/markings: CEJ, CEJ (in rectangular frame), 4, L/11, L/12, L/13, L/15, L/16, L/18, L/21, L/52 (in an oblong box)

The basic design is the same for each grade and takes the form of a Maltese Cross with a central, round plate embellished with a mobile

90

Photo 90 Coffins of the dead lying in state.

Photo 91 Spanish Cross with Swords – Bronze. The recess between the arms of the swastika are solid.

Photo 92 Spanish Cross with Swords – Silver. The recess between the arms of the swastika are rounded. This piece is struck in silver.

Photo 93 Spanish Cross with Swords – Gold. The recess between the arms of the swastika are rounded.

91

92

93

53

swastika. Through the quarters of the arms of the cross run double-edged swords with ornate hilts and quillons. Superimposed over these are finely detailed Luftwaffe flying eagles, clutching swastikas in their talons. There are two forms of the award which can conveniently be classed as the award piece and the second or LDO piece. The award measures 56mm across, with the width of the arms, taken across the points, being 23mm. The arms of the cross have a 1.5mm rim. The central, recessed fields produced by the rim are lightly pebbled. In the centre is a circle on which is placed a 15.5mm raised circular dish that has a 1mm raised edge line and a further similar line indented by 2mm.

All these measurements vary slightly between the two types and varying manufacturers and should be seen as a guide only. These measurements should be compared to the actual measurements in conjunction with the photographs illustrating this article.

The inner recessed central field has a raised swastika with the arms touching the circle. The fields of the tramline and the centre are lightly pebbled. The high parts of the medal are polished, while the pebbled areas are matt. The eagle emblems are separately struck and very neatly soldered to the arms of the cross. The eagles' tails can be encountered in a downward position as well as the more common extended form. The first form is indeed often encountered on reproductions but this fact alone should not influence the collector into deciding that an award so constructed is a reproduction.

The area between the arms of the swastika can be voided or solid depending upon the manufacturer. In the case of voided swastikas, it is only the lower portions that are found thus; the void in the arm adjacent to the claw is solid. This feature does not always indicate superior quality of manufacture. Beneath the eagles run two crossed swords with their hilts at the bottom of the cross. The swords are double-edged, have a central raised spine and a raised edge line on either side. They have a cross-guard with oblong box at the centre and quillons tapering from the edge to the central box. The quillons and box have a fine raised edge line and the recessed fields of the quillons have eight raised vertical lines, while the box has a vertical spine. The hilts are barrel-shaped, with small round pommels, and are wound with nine twists of twisted cord. The swords measure 62mm from the tip to the pommel and the cross-guard is 10mm across. The swords themselves are part of the stamping that forms the convex body of the cross. The reverse is plain and has a hinge, massive pin and C-form hook which is soldered directly to the lower arm of the cross.

Recently it seems greater store has been attributed to the award piece but in reality, which piece has the greater personal attachment and interest – the item presented and never worn or the second piece that was with the recipient at all times? Both types are of immense collecting interest and should surely be included in any serious collection.

One of the most reliable methods of identifying the award form as opposed to the second piece is the hinge, pin and hook assembly. The hinge on the award type is formed from an oblong plate that measures 11.5mm by 5mm and is 1.5mm thick. On the upper side is soldered a barrel hinge. The pin is then attached and lies over the plate, which forms the bed or stop for the pin to act against. The pin itself is normally bellied and drawn as opposed to having been sawn or die-struck from a blank piece of metal. The massive hook is of the C form and soldered directly to the middle of the bottom arm of the cross. The width of the hook is 3mm. In the case of the second piece the hinge is smaller and formed in one piece. It is attached to the body of the cross and rests on its side with the bellied pin resting across what is normally the bottom of the hinge. It measures 8mm by 5mm and is 3mm thick. The pin is normally sawn or stamped from a single piece of metal. The C-form hook in this case has an oblong profile. It is 2mm thick. A further form, which tends to be used on superior second pieces, has the hinge in an upright position, the pin is formed with a return at the hinge mount. This acts as the spring. The hook is a smaller, delicate C type.

The bronze class can be struck in bronze or silver that has been bronzed. The silver class can be found in varying silver grades, which are considered the award type, or bronze

crosses that have been silvered as the second or LDO pieces. The gold class can be in silver gilt. These are believed to be the actual award pieces, while plated or gilded bronze stampings are the second pieces. The grades of silver can be .800, .835, .900 and .925. However, there are massive tombac pieces produced by C.E. Juncker that are fire-gilded and these pieces are also considered to be award pieces. One such decoration was obtained in a grouping belonging to a naval officer along with his Spanish awards.

Photo 94 Spanish Cross without Swords – Bronze. The recess between the arms of the swastika are rounded.

Photo 95 Spanish Cross without Swords – Silver. The recess between the arms of the swastika are rounded.

Spanish Cross without Swords – Bronze and Silver Classes

Instituted: 14 April 1939
Number awarded: 7,869; 327
Rarity: scarce, very rare

Known maker(s)/markings: CEJ, CEJ (in rectangular frame), 4, L/11, L/12, L/13, L/15, L/16, L/18, L/21, L/52 (in an oblong box)

This badge is based on a Maltese Cross, as described in the section on the previous medals, but without swords, and in the quadrants are Luftwaffe eagles each clutching a segmented swastika in its talons. The cross is concave with a massive hinge, pin and hook on the reverse. The same observations about the hinge, pin and hook construction as described for the award type in the previous

decoration are relevant to this award. It was made in either bronze or silver. Those that were bronzed or left silver for that grade are considered to be the award type as are the massive bronze crosses. Those produced in bronze which were silvered to represent that grade are considered to be the second or private-purchase types. There was no Spanish Cross in Gold without Swords, although there is evidence that an order authorising it was issued.

The cross was rendered with an award document signed by Hitler. The regulations further prescribed that, upon the death of the recipient, the cross would remain in the possession of the family. They were awarded in a green box with burgundy lining, but blue boxes with blue liners and blue velvet bases along with deluxe domed maroon cases and green boxes with dove grey liners have been encountered. Examples with the LDO symbol or LDO stencilled in silver on the lid have been seen.

Spanish Cross in Gold with Diamonds

Instituted: 14 April 1939
Number awarded: 27
Rarity: extremely rare
Known maker(s)/markings:
J. Godet u. Sohn

This badge was produced in tombac and gilded. It takes the form of the preceding decorations but in this case the cross is more convex. The overall size of the badge is larger than the other pieces described. The height of the badge measured from point to point of the Maltese Cross is 60mm and the length of the swords is 65mm. The width across the points of the arms is 25mm. The swastikas clutched by the Luftwaffe eagles are segmented. The central plate with the diamonds measures 18.5mm. The arms of the cross are flat with a 2mm edge line polished and chamfered to the outer edge. The width of the metal the badge is constructed of is 2.5mm and the badge has a weight of 42 grams.

The pebbled parts are matt, these pebbled marks being hand raised. The raised portions of the other parts of the cross are highly polished. The centre, however, is quite different – it is a separately constructed plate, fixed to the body of the cross independently. The construction of this plate again was by hand and, in this case, the swastika's arms are broader and the circle surrounding it is also broader. Next to this circle are set fourteen rose-cut diamonds. There is no outer circle to the border of the diamonds, so that the actual facets and claw setting of the diamonds form the outer edge of the circle. The setting for these diamonds has been described in other references as silver but I would suggest that it is platinum, as it is in the other awards constructed in this manner to mount this type of diamond. The setting could also be produced in white gold.

The reverse has a large pin, hinge and hook construction. This is fixed at the upper arm of the cross with a large hook secured to the middle of the bottom arm. The hinge is formed from an oblong plate that measures 11.5mm x 3.5mm and is 2mm thick, with the barrel of the hinge attached to the upper edge of the plate. The pin is hand-sawn with a slightly bellied profile and rests over the oblong plate. The hook is of C-form and is 2mm thick. The central device is held on to the cross by a disc on the reverse, which is slightly convex, which mirrors the front plate and has two open rivets protruding through it (in other words there is a small hole down the centre of the rivet, which allows the outer edge to be hammered over from the centre). On this plate, hand-engraved in flowing script, is 'J. Godet & Sohn. K.G.' and underneath, 'Unter dem Linden'. Beneath this in the centre, in larger Arabic numerals, is '53'.

This award was to be worn on the right breast pocket of the uniform.

The box for this award has been described as a white box covered with calfskin, with a gold line round the lid. This box is square with rounded corners and was produced with a white flock base and lid liner. It has also been stated by authoritative sources that some boxes were similar to the blue boxes in which the standard crosses were awarded.

With the award a dress copy or second piece was supposedly presented. This I have titled A Type and will discuss it later in the chapter.

This badge was instituted on 14 April 1939. The precise criteria for the award are a little obscure but it would seem it was given to commanders and particularly successful pilots of the Condor Legion. Hitler took it upon himself to award this decoration personally to the twenty-five original recipients upon their return from Spain. Recipients of the Military Medal with Diamonds from the Spanish were to be awarded the Spanish Cross in Gold with Diamonds. The three commanders of the Condor Legion – Sperrle, Volkmann and Richthofen – were awarded the special class of the Spanish medal and thus should have been the only recipients of this class of the Spanish Cross. However, Hitler chose to retain the prerogative of presenting it to those combatants deserving of it in his opinion.

The known recipients were:

Oberleutnant Wilhelm Balthasar	J-88
Oberleutnant Otto Bertram	J-88
Leutnant Wilhelm Boddem	J-88
Oberleutnant Kraft Eberhard	J-88
Oberleutnant Wilhelm Ensslen	J-88
Leutnant Paul Fehlhaber	Ln-88
Oberleutnant Adolf Galland	J-88
Hauptmann Harro Harder	J-88
Major Martin Harlinghausen	AS-88
Leutnant Oskar Henrici	J-88
Oberleutnant Max Graf Hoyos	K-88

Oberleutnant Hans-Detlef von Kassel   A-88

Hauptmann Günther Lützow   J-88

Oberleutnant Karl Mehnert   K-88

Hauptmann Werner Mölders   J-88

Hauptmann Rudolf Freiherr   K-88
von Moreau

Hauptmann Wolfgang Neudörffer   K-88

Oberleutnant Walter Oesau   J-88

Generalleutnant Wolfram Freiherr   S-88
von Richthofen

Leutnant Heinz Runze   A-88

Hauptmann Wolfgang Schellmann   J-88

Hauptmann Joachim Schlichting   J-88

Oberleutnant Reinhard Seiler   J-88

General der Flieger Hugo Sperrle   S-88

Oberleutnant Bernhard Stärcke   K-88

General der Flieger Helmut Volkmann   S-88

Major Karl-Heinz Wolff   AS-88

However, David Littlejohn and Dr Klietmann both state in their books that there were 28 recipients. This further recipient is believed to be Oberstleutnant von Thoma who is also noted as having received the Spanish Military Medal with Diamonds. It has also been stated, but is as yet unsubstantiated, that in contradiction to the accepted belief that there were only three recipients of that medal, the whole of the remaining twenty-three also received this award.

An interesting progression in the grades of the crosses occurred some 14 days after the lavish reception held in the great hall of the new Reich Chancellery, where Hitler entertained Spanish dignitaries and fifty to sixty holders of the Spanish Cross in Gold with Swords and a dozen holders of the Spanish Cross with Diamonds. Adolf Galland and Wilhelm Balthasar, who both held the Spanish Cross in Gold with Swords and had been at the reception, were summoned to Göring's summer home by the North Sea, where he announced that they were to be awarded the highest German award for participation in the Spanish Civil War. They were both then instructed to remove their crosses and hand them to him, whereupon he presented them with their diamond awards. Galland later recalled that Göring kept the original crosses in his pocket and he also stated that he only received one cross, the standard award piece.

Spanish Cross in Gold with Diamonds – Dress Copy

I have encountered three distinct forms of the Spanish Cross in Gold with Diamonds – Dress Copy, which I have coded as A Type, B Type and C Type. The A and B Type I have observed on three occasions and the C Type is unique. As this was a private-purchase piece and variations do occur in the construction of such badges, it is difficult to write with finality as to their status. It is not known whether every recipient purchased an example for general wear or if private-purchase examples were issued on certain occasions to the original recipient. However, the A Type was supposed to have been presented in conjunction with the award type of cross and two of the examples I have encountered were presented to, or owned, by Major Martin Harlinghausen and Hauptmann Günther Lützow. Contemporary photographs also seem to show that the A Type was the form that was widely worn. Oberleutnant Walter Oesau was photographed on many occasions wearing what appears to be the A Type.

Spanish Cross in Gold with Diamonds – Dress Copy – A Type

Rarity: extremely rare
Known maker(s)/markings: L/12, CEJ

The A Type is found in two forms. These are so similar as not to justify a separate category. The first is produced from a standard cross and measures 57mm in width and 23mm across the tips of the arms. The thickness of the metal that produces the cross is 2mm and the badge weighs 34 grams. The centre has a diamond setting reminiscent of the award type but, in this case, the claw settings holding the diamonds make an irregular outer edge, while the inner edge of the setting has a 2mm flat line. The width of the total setting is 21mm. It is placed over the central plate that has the mobile swastika and the 2mm flat line serves as the edge that surrounds the swastika. The length of the swords is 63mm. The Luftwaffe eagles are delicate and stylised and hold swastikas in their claws. These swastikas have voided arms only on the left and right. The outer edge of the diamond settings obscures the view of the lower portion of the swastikas.

98

99

100

Photo 98 Spanish Cross in Gold with Diamonds – Dress Copy A-Type.

Photo 99 Spanish Cross in Gold with Diamonds – Dress Copy A-Type (reverse).

Photo 100 Spanish Cross in Gold with Diamonds – Dress Copy B-Type.

The reverse is similar to the standard piece. It has a massive hinge, pin and C-form hook soldered to an oval plate, which is fixed to the bottom arm of the cross, just above the point of the V of the lower arm. The construction of the hinge and pin is as described in the discussion of the award pieces of the standard Spanish Cross. The central diamond setting is held on to the reverse by a circular plate that mirrors the inner plate of the obverse and measures 13.5mm. This has two protrusions on either side, which are drilled and through which are placed two large rivets that are penned over. In the centre of the plate and struck directly on to the reverse of the cross is the maker's mark in an oblong box, 'CEJ' or 'L/12'. The whole of the reverse is very finely matted giving a dull gold effect.

The second form is likewise produced from a standard cross and measures 57mm in width and 23mm across the tips of the arms. The thickness of the cross is 2.5mm and the badge weighs 42 grams. The centre has a similar

setting to the first form, with the inner edge of the setting measuring 2mm. The width of the total setting is 23.5mm. In this case, the setting is placed lower on the cross and thus the inner 2mm edge forms a larger circle round the mobile swastika, which is now at the same height as the 2mm line. The line on the plate surrounding the swastika is visible with a small 0.5mm gap between it and the 2mm inner setting line, producing a tramline effect. The length of the swords is 63.5mm. The Luftwaffe eagles are slightly larger and pronounced in design. The swastikas have three of the arms voided. The eagle and swastika emblem is soldered further up the arms of the cross so in this case the swastikas

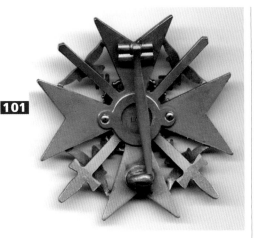

101

are not partially obscured by the diamond setting. The diamonds are marginally larger to produce the circle, rather than increasing the number of diamonds.

The reverse is similar to the first form save that the hinge is of the type that lies on its side and the pin is stamped from a piece of sheet metal. The central diamond setting is held to the reverse by a circular plate that mirrors the inner plate of the obverse and measures 14.5mm. The rest of the construction is as described in the first form. In the centre of the plate and struck directly on to the reverse of the cross is the maker's mark 'L/12'. The whole of the reverse is smooth and the gilding has a satin appearance.

Spanish Cross in Gold with Diamonds – Dress Copy – B Type

Known maker(s)/markings: unmarked

I have encountered the B Type of cross in two distinct forms. Both forms are similar to that of the award type, save for the central ring, which is formed in two parallel circles. The swastika in this version is at the same height as the two circles, with its points touching the inside of the smaller circle. The field produced between the circle's edge and the arms of the swastika is pebbled, as is the field between the two lines. The first has twelve white sapphires. The second has fourteen, which are smaller in

size and number to the diamonds in the awarded type. They also fit directly between those two lines, which give a completely different appearance to the centre of this award. The plate on to which the swastika and sapphires are set is fixed to the body of the cross by two ball rivets. The first form has the swastikas that are held in the Luftwaffe eagle's talons unsegmented, while the other has the swastikas with the lower three arms voided. The measurements of both these badges were not made available to me but can be presumed to be that of the normal award cross.

The cross and the plate are made of silver and the reverse sometimes has the hallmark applied between the two rivets. It has a large pin with a hinge fixed to the upper arm. The lower one has a large retaining hook. The whole of the badge is gilded and produced in a very high quality.

The precise nature of this award is unknown but it must be presumed that these pieces are museum display pieces or tailor's shop pieces. The second piece described is in the collection of Jim Hingley who obtained it from a US veteran who acquired it in Italy with other rare items.

Spanish Cross in Gold with Diamonds – Dress Copy – C Type

Known maker(s)/markings: unmarked

The C Type is also produced from a standard cross and measures 58mm across and 23mm across the tips of the arms. The outer line running round the arms measures 2mm and is gently chamfered to the outer edges. The central diamond setting measures 17.5mm and the claws in this case have only a very finely serrated appearance to the edge. The inner line setting is 1mm and this allows the swastika to be more pronounced. The badge weighs 41 grams. The swastikas held in the Luftwaffe eagle's talons have all their arms voided.

The reverse is plain and shows no sign of where the central diamond setting is attached to the body of the cross. It has a small barrel hinge and square tapering pin and C-form hook that is attached directly to the body of

the cross. The pin has a round ball at the point. At the centre of the cross is the silver content, '800' and on the pin is a further '800' intaglio. This badge is purported to have belonged to Generalmajor von Richthofen and was supposedly a personal gift from General Franco.

This badge was contained in a red box with maroon silk lid liner and matching maroon velvet base. The upper lid has an oblong gilded silver plate that has, in hand-engraved Gothic script, in two lines, 'Kampfgeschwader Boelcke', placed over the arms of the swastika. The inside of the lid has the Luftwaffe flying eagle. The other forms of boxes are unknown but it is assumed that they were just the manufacturer's or jeweller's protective cases.

Cross of Honour for the Relatives of the Dead in Spain

Instituted: 14 April 1939
Number awarded: 315
Rarity: very rare
Known maker(s)/markings:
J. Godet u. Sohn

The cross is constructed of bronze or bronzed silver taking the same form as the breast crosses but is smaller. It measures 44mm across, with the width of the arms, taken across the points, being 17mm. The arms of the cross have a 1.25mm rim. The central

Photo 101 Spanish Cross in Gold with Diamonds – Dress Copy B-Type (reverse).

Photo 102 Spanish Cross in Gold with Diamonds – Dress Copy C-Type.

Photo 103 Spanish Cross in Gold with Diamonds – Dress Copy C-Type (reverse).

recessed fields produced by the rim are lightly pebbled. In the centre is a circle, on which is placed a 14mm raised circular dish with a 0.5mm raised edge line and a further similar line indented by 1.5mm. The cross weighs 13 grams. At the top is a ring for the suspension ribbon, which can also be encountered with the normal round ouse or an elongated form. There are two forms of eagle and swastika emblem found in the quarters of the arms of the cross. The first eagle has a downswept tail reminiscent of that found on the ribbon emblem used to denote the Luftwaffe on the military long-service awards. The swastika is also solid on this form. The second type has the eagle with the extended tail. The swastika can be found with both voided and solid arms. The ribbon is 30mm wide and consists of the German and Spanish national colours, with thin outer vertical stripes of red, yellow, red, yellow, red, white and a wide central stripe of black to represent mourning.

Boddem, Harri Büttner, Willi Deriesch, Albert Echart, Werner Fischer, Friedrich Haerle, Rudolf Kollenda, Walter Lange, Alexander Mertes, Paul Pawelcik and Hans Schrödel.

The award was to be worn at all times and, in the case of men, it was fixed over the left breast pocket. Usually it is found on a court-mounted ribbon, that is to say the ribbon is furled below the medal and the reverse of the ribbon is padded, the whole item being formed on a metal plate with its own individual pin mounting at the top. The medal is usually found clipped on to a hook, which enables the ring of the medal to be easily removed. For women, the ribbon was formed into a bow.

As far as the award documents are concerned, it is worth mentioning that the presentation folder of some of the documents was in the form of a leather case. This indicated the high prestige value placed on them. Leather cases were issued with the documents of only a few of the highest decorations. In this case the folders were made of dark blue synthetic leather by a Frau Emma Gerhardt in Jena. On the front, they carry the words, 'Ehrenkreuz für Hinterbliebene deutscher Spanienkämpfer' (Cross of honour for surviving dependants of German fighters in Spain) in gold letters in four lines. Above this, is a golden oak branch with four leaves and one acorn. When closed, the folder measures approximately 22.5cm x 32.5cm.

The box to this award is an oblong green case with an off-white liner and an embossed representation of the cross on the lid.

An interesting theory has been put forward that this cross was found in the relevant grades of the award of the Spanish Cross and therefore there was a bronze, silver and gold class. These were to represent the class of the cross that the recipient's fallen relative had gained.

The reverse is concave and plain.

This medal was announced on 14 April 1939 and was to honour those who had fallen in combat, died as a consequence of wounds received in combat, who died as a result of illness or disease directly caused by wounds, died due to illness or accident sustained while serving in Spain or Spanish Morocco, or who were listed as missing in action in that conflict. There were rules governing which family member should receive the award, and in the event of that person's death the award passed to the next in line on the original list.

The known recipients were: those killed on the *Deutschland* and Ulrich Bonisch, Wilhelm

Christian von Tettinek has informed me that he has encountered the diamond grade on two occasions. The theory seems to have validity for it does appear incongruous to give different grades to the living but for 'fallen heroes' to be commemorated with only a bronze form. This is also reinforced by the issuing of the leather folder similar to those given to the next of kin of holders of some of the highest awards. However, the converse to the argument must surely be that all the fallen heroes were equal; their sacrifice would be honoured similarly, creating an equal 'brotherhood of remembrance'.

Spanish Wound Badge – Black, Silver and Gold Classes

Instituted: 22 May 1939
Number awarded: Bronze 182; Silver 1; Gold 0
Rarity: scarce, scarce, rare
Known maker(s)/markings: unmarked

This badge was introduced on 22 May 1939, by order of Adolf Hitler, renewing the 1918 status of the military wound badge. The World War 1 naval wound badge was not reinstituted. The regulations stated that the badge would be awarded to German personnel who had received wounds in action in Spain. The badge consists of a wreath of laurel leaves with a bow at its base and five berries, or dots, at its apex. The central device of the badge is a World War 1 steel helmet surmounting crossed swords, with a swastika stamped into the helmet from the reverse. The field is pebbled but some examples of the badge have this field cut out, leaving the swords and helmet in silhouette.

The reverse of the badge follows the design of the obverse, as the badge is stamped out. However, one example I have examined of the silver grade is stamped out as previously described and is then attached to a backing plate. This gives the impression of the badge being formed in a solid manner. This badge is constructed in real silver. A further example has been encountered in gold that is similarly constructed but with a broad blade pin and having two small blowholes situated beneath it. This badge is very lightweight, finely struck and superbly made. The pin to all the badges encountered is usually of a needle design.

The criteria for the award were:

1. One or two wounds – black award

2. Three or four wounds – silver award

3. Five or more wounds – gold award

At this point it is important to dispel some of the misconceptions surrounding the award of this badge. The point to remember when identifying an original Spanish wound badge is that one manufacturer produced the awards. The originals were made from the die of a World War 1 Wound Badge to which a swastika was added. The badge has a high swastika, which has sharply defined edges at a 90-degree angle and the top of the swastika was flush with the surface of the helmet. There were considerably more manufactured than required. They are not to be confused with the later 1st Type 1939 Wound Badge. This design of badge continued to be awarded until at least 1942.

The badge came in a black box with a cream flock lining.

It is also possible that original recipients of the badges awarded for Spain could, for subsequent wounds sustained in the World War 2 receive the higher grade in this form. This theory has been denied in other reference books but it is highly possible that this practice was applied. One such story has been encountered, where a Panzer crewman, Heinrich Schell, had received the badge in black for being wounded twice in Spain. Subsequently, he was wounded in the 1939 Polish campaign. He then fought on the Western Front in 1940 and lost a lower part of his leg. For this wound he received the Wound Badge 1939 Gold

Class. However, while convalescing in hospital, his commanding officer visited him and upon seeing his Gold 1939 Wound Badge commented that he should have the Spanish type and subsequently gave him such an example. This was purchased from the recipient and is now in my collection. The quality of the badge is very poor and does not give the impression of the calibre that the presentation warranted. Quite likely this was nothing more than a one-off piece of camaraderie.

Photo 107 Spanish Wound Badge – Silver.

Photo 108 Reverse of Spanish Wound Badge – Silver.

Photo 109 Spanish Wound Badge – Silver Miniature.

Photo 110 Reverse of Spanish Wound Badge – Silver Miniature.

Photo 111 Spanish Wound Badge – Gold. These were never produced or awarded for the war. They are struck as the first wound badges of World War 2.

Photo 112 Reverse of the Spanish Wound Badge – Gold. This shows the blow hole. The badge is a thin pressing with a thicker back plate attached.

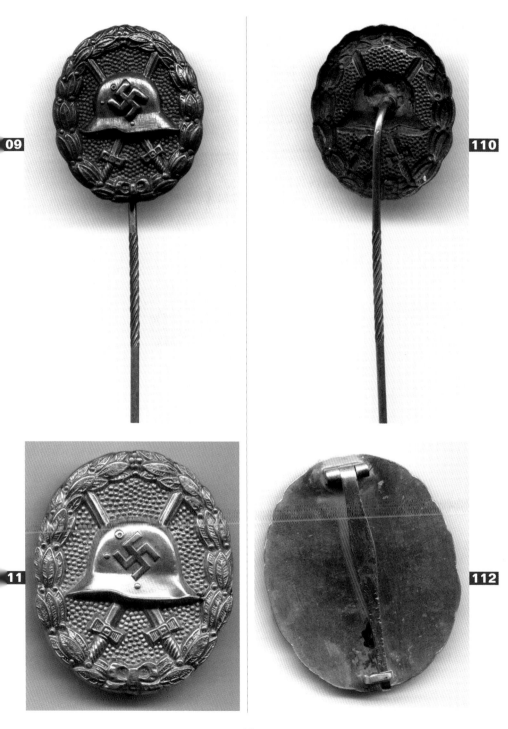

Cuff titles

Cuff titles, or as they are also known, sleeve bands, were worn for a number of purposes, but primarily to denote membership in elite units or specially designated formations. Personnel assigned to the staff of certain schools were also recognised by the grant of a cuff band. They were also employed as awards to commemorate a campaign.

Africa – Theatre of Operations Cuff Band

Instituted: 25 February 1942
Rarity: scarce
Known maker(s)/markings: unmarked

On 18 July 1941 a cuff title 'AFRIKA KORPS' was authorised for wear by members of this unit who were fighting on the continent of Africa, by the Army Commander-in-Chief, Field Marshal von Brauchitsch. Further orders (HV 41A, Nos 496 and 778, dated 18 July 1941 and 4 November 1941) permitted naval personnel of all units attached to the Afrika Korps, or to the later Panzerarmee Afrika to wear cuff titles of the Army pattern. These were never intended to be considered as awards but just purely to provide unit recognition. On their return from Africa, some servicemen continued to wear these cuff titles on an unofficial basis.

The cuff title is a cotton band 33mm wide with 'AFRIKA KORPS' in silver block lettering on a dark green background, edged at the top and bottom with a band of silver embroidery 0.3cm wide. These silver bands are themselves edged in a tan-coloured material. The whole of this cuff title was in fact woven as one integral piece. This title was worn on the right cuff of service, field service, and uniform tunics as well as on greatcoats. The cuff title was officially permitted to be worn on the European continent when the man was on leave there. A minimum of two months' service in Africa was required before being allowed to wear the cuff title. It was worn 15cm from the bottom of the field tunic and tropical tunic sleeve, 1cm above the cuff of the greatcoat and 7.5cm above the field grey tunic cuff.

Kreta Commemorative Cuff Title

Instituted: 16 October 1942
Rarity: rare
Known maker(s)/markings: unmarked

On 16 October 1942 this award was introduced to reward all personnel of the Army, Navy and Luftwaffe who had participated or helped in the capture of the island of Crete in May 1941.

This cuff band is a white cotton strip, 33mm wide, with a border of yellow cotton. In between the borders is embroidered the name 'KRETA' in yellow cotton. On either side of the name is a sprig of acanthus leaves in a stylised pattern. This can be found in two distinct types: the normal issue band with a seven-leaf cone and a superior quality band with the cone being formed from nine individual leaves. In the past reference works have suggested that the only material in which the band was produced was off-white cotton, but there was a variation of this cuff title, of which original examples have

Photo 113: Africa – Theatre of Operation Cuff Band.

Photo 114: Kreta Commemorative Cuff Title.

Photo 115: 'Afrika' Commemorative Cuff Title.

'Afrika' Commemorative Cuff Title

Instituted: 15 January 1943
Rarity: scarce
Known maker(s)/markings: unmarked

been found, produced on an off-white felt strip. These are very scarce. Careful scrutiny and great caution must be exercised when deciding the originality, as a number of reproductions of this award have been produced in this material.

The award was to have been worn on all uniforms including overcoats or greatcoats. No awards were made after 31 October 1944. The criteria for the award were:

1. To have been engaged in a glider or parachute landing, between 20 and 27 May 1941 on the island of Crete.

2. To have been engaged in air operations over Crete during the period of invasion.

3. In the case of the Navy, to have been engaged on active service up to 27 May 1941, in the Cretan theatre of operations.

4. Army personnel who had put to sea on 19 May 1941 in the naval light flotilla.

An official cuff title was introduced to replace the unofficial wearing of the Africa – Theatre of Operations cuff band titles on 15 January 1943. This cuff title was a khaki-coloured band, 33mm wide, with a border on each edge of silver-coloured cotton. In the centre of this band was embroidered, also in silver-coloured cotton, the word 'AFRIKA' flanked by a stylised palm tree on each side. (A palm tree with a swastika midway up the trunk had been the sign of the Afrika Korps.) Another form has been encountered with a khaki cotton band measuring 44mm. This was turned over and the top and bottom edges machine-stitched with pale green cotton to fix them. On to the centre of the band is placed a strip of off-white cotton stitched directly to the band. The upper and lower borders are 33mm wide and on the central field produced is embroidered, in silver bullion wire, the title 'AFRIKA'. This is flanked on either side by a palm tree, again in bullion wire. Each of the five fronds has a black cotton central line. The purpose of this band is unknown and it can only be considered as an officer's private-purchase piece. There is also a version with a blue band, edged in gold, with gold palm trees and title

as before. The purpose of this type of cuff title is unknown but one theory is that it was produced to reward naval personnel. One such sleeve band was presented to a senior petty officer Heinz Ubinger in May 1943 for service in Tunis while assigned to a Luftwaffe ground unit. Konteradmiral Wilhelm Meendsen-Böhlken, commander of naval forces in Italy, is pictured wearing a hand-embroidered Afrika cuff title as described. After 29 August 1944, with the exception of prisoners of war, those missing in action and personnel confined to hospital due to infectious diseases who could possibly on recovery be returned to active service, no more Afrika titles were to be awarded.

The criteria for the award were:

1. A minimum of six months on North African soil.

2. Being wounded in combat in the North African theatre, on land, on the waters around North Africa or in the air.

3. Contraction of an illness while in the North African theatre. This was to include personnel evacuated to the continent of Europe due to that illness but service had to have been in excess of three months before contracting the illness for the possible recipient to be considered for an award of the cuff title under those circumstances.

4. On 6 May 1943, Hitler decreed that the qualifying service time regarding the final phases of the campaign was to be reduced to four months.

5. Recipients of decorations awarded in this theatre of operations, to include the

Iron Cross, German Cross in Gold, Goblet of Honour or Salver of Honour, would automatically be awarded the cuff title regardless of the length of service time spent in Africa.

6. Death of a member of the Afrika Korps in the line of duty automatically qualified him for an award of the cuff title without serving the time requirement. In this case the next of kin received the award document.

'Kurland' Commemorative Cuff Title

Instituted: 12 March 1945
Rarity: very rare
Known maker(s)/markings: unmarked

On 12 March 1945 Hitler introduced a cuff title to reward the defenders of the besieged Courland region of Latvia. In early 1945 General Schörner of Army Group Courland had recommended to Hitler that all members of his command should be decorated for their heroic stand. However, due to wartime shortages of materials, a decoration in the form of a Courland Shield was not adopted.

This cuff title was produced locally, in a weaving mill at Kuldiga. The band is of unusual design as the reverse has a form of cross-stitch joining the two outer edges together, these outer edges having been turned over. The obverse has a bold black edge beneath which is a line of black oblong dots. Beneath these is a fine thin black line. Between these two thin lines, in capitals, is the legend, 'KURLAND'. Before the K is a shield with a black cross as its central motif, which is not unlike a Balkan Cross. The shield is square-topped with a pointed base. This shield is, in

fact, the crest of the Grand Master of the Teutonic Knights. The other side has a similar shield but in this case it is black, with a white moose's head looking inwards to the left from the viewer's position, this being the coat of arms of Mitau (now Jelgava in Latvia). The overall colour of the band is off-white and the material is of rough cotton.

The history behind this cuff title is unusual. In October 1944 the bulk of Army Group North under Generaloberst Ferdinand Schörner became encircled by the Soviet forces in the Courland region of Latvia. There followed what became known as the six great battles of Courland. At the time of the first battle, which raged between 16 and 20 October, there were thirty-four German divisions in Courland The army group, then redesignated Army Group Courland, comprised some 400,000 men, 12,000 of whom were SS and police. A number of German formations were subsequently pulled out and shipped home across the Baltic but such heavy losses were suffered by the rest that a report of 1 April 1945 showed a German strength of only nineteen divisions, some of which were reduced to mere battalion or even company size. These units held at bay over 120 fully equipped and fresh Soviet divisions. Schörner was promoted to Generalfeldmarschall for his leadership and awarded the Oak Leaves, Swords and Diamonds to the Knight's Cross.

On 3 May 1945, at 19.30 hours, the new Führer, Grossadmiral Dönitz, ordered the long-awaited evacuation of military personnel from the Courland Peninsula. A few managed to escape in a Dunkirk-style operation but most were trapped when the armistice was signed on 8 May 1945.

The precise criteria for the award are a little vague but generally take the same form as that for the Afrika cuff band. The award was also to be used as a campaign commemorative title for those who had been engaged in the battles for Courland. The cuff title saw actual distribution by the end of April 1945 with the allocation going firstly to the enlisted personnel, then the non-commissioned officers, then the officers. Awards were made right up to and including 8 May 1945.

Photo 116: 'Afrika' Commemorative Cuff Title. This example is hand embroidered and was probably a private enterprise during the Africa conflict.

Photo 117: 'Kurland' Commemorative Cuff Title.

Photo 118: Reverse of the 'Kurland' Commemorative Cuff Title showing the crude method of hand weaving employed.

Arm Shields Common to All Services

Of all the awards of the Third Reich these were a totally new innovation, and had been brought into existence to reward the personnel of the armed forces, or people in their employ. The shields recorded service in a theatre of operations and were not necessarily to reward heroism or valour, although if a decoration was awarded the recipient received the arm shield for that theatre of operations. They were produced in metal, which was stamped out of a thin sheet and was usually fixed to a cloth backing corresponding to the uniform colour of the branch of the service to which the recipient belonged. The cloth backing enabled the recipient to sew it easily on to the tunic. These shields were worn on the left arm and when two were awarded they were worn with the first above the second, separated by a small, approximately 5mm gap. In the case of the Waffen SS the shield had to be worn above the SS arm eagle. In the unlikely event of three shields being awarded, the recipient placed, or attempted to place, the last two shields side by side, with a 5mm gap between them and the first one that was awarded, so that when one looked at the wearer's arm the shields were in the form of a triangle. It was permitted to wear the shields on service, walking-out and guard uniforms and greatcoats. They could be worn on the uniforms of any of the party organisations, though this was rare, except in the case of fighting troops who had been invalided out of the armed forces. There is no recorded instance of the shields described in this section being produced in a cloth version. This seems strange as they were bulky to wear and a cloth version would have been logical.

Narvik Shield – Silver and Gold Class

Instituted: 19 August 1940
Number awarded: Silver 8,577; Gold 3,661
Rarity: scarce, scarce
Known maker(s)/markings: unmarked

This shield was instituted on 19 August 1940. It is pointed at the bottom and surmounted at the top by three lines. The first protrudes beyond the shield's edges, the second is in line with the edges and the third is short of the outline of the badge. On this rests an eagle, head to the viewer's left, with exaggerated downswept wings. Its claws clutch a wreath surrounding a swastika. The body of the shield has a box with the word 'NARVIK' and beneath this is the date '1940'. The main design of the badge is a crossed single-bladed propeller and anchor, surmounted by edelweiss. These were the symbols of the three arms (Luftwaffe, Kriegsmarine and mountain troops) of the German fighting forces employed in the capture of Norway. Professor Richard Klein of Munich designed the awards.

This shield was unique in that it was produced in two forms. The silver grade was given to the Army and Luftwaffe, with a backing cloth corresponding to the branch of the service to which the recipient belonged. The gold one was awarded solely to the Kriegsmarine and therefore should only be found with a navy blue backing. However, gilt examples are occasionally encountered on field grey cloth worn by Narvik veterans who served in the marine artillery and wore field-grey Army-style uniforms. At least one example is known of a Narvik naval veteran, Karl Wilhelm Krause, who had been Hitler's personal orderly and bodyguard from 1934 to 1939. He had joined the Kriegsmarine in 1931 and three years later Hitler had chosen him from a line-up of other naval prospects. In September 1939, after a petty squabble over some spring water that he had represented to Hitler as bottled mineral water (which, incidentally, was Hitler's favourite drink), the Führer sacked him. During the war, Krause served briefly in the Kriegsmarine, then as an aide in the Reich Chancellery and finally as a

Photo 119: Narvik Shield – Gold Class.

Army
2. Gebirgs-Division 206
3. Gebirgs-Division 2,338
others 59
posthumous 152

Luftwaffe
Aircrew 1,309
paratroopers 756
posthumous 96

Navy
Destroyers 2,672
others 115;
posthumous 410

Merchant Navy
442
posthumous 22

The naval form had its prescribed method of wear laid down by order MV 40, No 674, dated 12 September 1940, as on the left upper sleeve of the greatcoat, frock coat, reefer and pea jacket, blue shirt of the blue uniform and of the greatcoat and tunic of the field-grey uniform. Wear on mess and dress jackets and white shirts of junior NCOs and privates were not permitted until after the end of the war. An additional order of 30 January 1941 (MV 41, No 60) regulated the wear above the sleeve rank insignia of junior NCOs and privates. Each recipient was issued with three copies of the shield and could purchase additional examples through retail outlets by producing his proof of entitlement.

Cholm Shield

Instituted: 1 July 1942
Number awarded: 5,500 approx
Rarity: very rare
Known maker(s)/markings: unmarked

This shield was introduced on 1 July 1942. It is made of white metal with a flat top and pointed bottom and is 65mm high by 40mm wide. The central design is an open-winged eagle, clutching an Iron Cross in its talons, the centre of which has a disproportionately large swastika relative to the size of the Iron Cross.

captain in an SS Panzer flak unit, credited with shooting down 45 allied aircraft. Krause was personally awarded the German Cross in Gold by Hitler. From photographic evidence it is clear that he wore the gilt Narvik Shield on both his field-grey uniform and black Panzer jacket.

The total number of silver awards was 8,577 – 2,755 to the Army, 2,161 to the Luftwaffe and 3,661 to the Navy. These can be further broken down to the component units.

120

Beneath this is the word 'CHOLM' and then the date of award '1942'. Polizei Rottwachtmeister Schlimmer, an NCO of the Police Reserve Battalion serving in the area, was encouraged by the local commander, Generalmajor Scherer, to draw up a design for this shield, which was slightly longer than the adopted form, with the eagle's head facing to the right. This design was submitted for consideration and, after minor changes by Professor Klein of Munich, was approved by Hitler for production.

There are two forms of this shield, the design of which varies slightly. This variation can be seen most clearly in the lettering and the date. The edge rim is also slightly more pronounced on the second type. Other general differences lie in the cloth backing. The first type extends above and below the shield equally with a semi-circular profile. The cloth is coarse and a field-grey colour. The reverse has three pins, two at the top and one below, in the middle. The backing paper is usually dark grey to black. The second type has a cloth backing that follows the outline of the shield. The cloth is of an open felt type and a more green hue. The reverse has four pins, positioned two at the top and two directly underneath at the bottom. The paper backing is normally a light brown-red and often has the number '2,40' in pencil.

It has been stated that the early production pieces were struck in lightweight metal and were backed with the first type large oval cloth

to have been made on this form of badge. The explanation for the second type would fit most comfortably to these units, for I was most fortunate to obtain from the family of Lieutenant-Commander Albert McRae, part of the Kiel naval headquarters brick library, which included an example of the second type shield. The colour of the backing also matches that of the naval field-grey dress.

The shield was instituted was to reward the troops who held a defensive pocket that had been created at Cholm, a small town on the Lovat River in the Kalinin region of Russia in the winter of 1941/2. These included Army grenadiers, artillery, mounted units and Gebirgsjäger, a police reserve battalion and elements of a naval transport unit. The commander was General-major Scherer. Hitler ordered that the pocket be defended to the last man; no retreat was to be countenanced. Despite cold, hunger and typhus, the garrison held out against overwhelming odds until relieved on 5 May 1942.

To reward this achievement, Scherer received the Oak Leaves to the Knight's Cross and he made the awards to 5,500 assorted men from various units who defended the pocket. There was an improvised airstrip within the pocket and Luftwaffe crews who landed there were eligible for the award. The last award for this shield was 1 April 1943.

patch, while later examples, which would have been sold through LDO outlets, were in non-magnetic zinc and mounted on shield-shaped backing cloth. The two examples that I have used for research were both struck from base metal, which then had a silver wash applied. The first type is struck with a slightly convex profile, while the second is flat. The cloth backing measures 102mm by 62mm and 78mm by 54mm, with most of the examples being in these two types and blue Luftwaffe backing being rarely encountered. It has also been suggested that examples may exist on navy blue backing, as naval transport units did operate on the Lovat River at Cholm. However, as these troops wore field-grey dress in normal service, such awards were unlikely

Crimea Shield

Instituted: 25 July 1942
Number awarded: 100,000 approx
Rarity: scarce
Known maker(s)/markings: J.F.S. 1942

This is a bronze shield with an Army eagle at the top, the wings just breaking the edge of the shield, and the talons clutching a wreath surrounding a swastika. On either side of the wreath are the dates '1941' and '1942' respectively. Beneath this is a map of the Crimean region, with the major rivers and six towns marked on it. The word 'Krim' (German for

122

cut in the edges to secure the clips. In this case there is sometimes no cloth backing provided. When it comes with a cloth backing, the four semi-circular lugs are pressed through the cloth and then retained by the back plate, which is then covered by a paper backing. The third form is struck from a slightly thicker plate and has a much less well-defined design. The reverse has three pins, two at the top and one directly beneath, in the middle at the bottom.

The shield was promulgated in July 1942 with the following telegram from Hitler to the commander of the forces in the Crimea, General Erich von Manstein:

Crimea) is impressed on to this map. This shield was produced from a thin ferrous plate and stamped with the design. It then had an olive bronze finish applied and was artificially patinated.

It was authorised for wear on virtually all forms of uniforms, to include white summer dress, tan tropical dress and the brown uniform of the Nazi Party. The most common was the field grey of the Army. Each soldier was eligible for five examples of the shield. In the case of posthumous awards one shield, accompanied by the possession certificate, was sent to the next of kin. It is estimated that over 100,000 awards of this shield were rendered during the period of award.

There are three distinct methods of production encountered in both this and the Kuban Shield (see below). The first is a finely detailed badge fixed to a cloth backing corresponding to the colour of the branch of service to which the recipient belonged. This cloth backing measures 75mm by 65mm. The reverse has four prongs, two at the top and two directly beneath at the bottom. The whole is covered by a black paper backing. The second form has a less finely defined design with two lugs on the vertical sides of the shield. These are bent over to secure a thin metal back plate. This plate has four notches

'In thankful appreciation of your particular merit in the victorious battle for the Crimea, with the destruction of Kerch and the overcoming of the natural and powerful man-made defences of the Sevastopol fortress, I promote you to field marshal. With your promotion and through the institution of a commemorative shield for all Crimea combatants, I honour, on behalf of the entire German people, the heroic achievements of the troops under your command.'

The badge was to reward the troops engaged in operations in this region from 21 September 1941 to 4 July 1942. Romanian troops serving with distinction in the Crimea were also eligible for the award.

The criteria for the award were one or more of:

1. To have served in the region for three months;

2. To have taken part in at least one major combat operation;

3. To have been wounded whilst serving in that region.

Crimea Shield - Gold Class

Instituted: 1 July 1942
Number awarded: 2
Rarity: extremely rare
Known maker(s)/markings: unmarked

This grade of Crimean Shield was awarded twice and the badge was produced in real gold. The first award was made to Marshal Antonescu of Rumania, which he received on 3 July 1943 in Bucharest from Manstein in recognition of the part played by the Rumanian divisions deployed in the campaign. The second was to Manstein himself, which he received from the members of his staff on his birthday, 24 November 1943. Manstein also used the design of the Crimea Shield as his personal emblem painted on his aircraft and personal vehicles. The exact number of shields produced is not known but it is assumed that more than two examples were made, as photographs show Manstein wearing the shield both on his tunic and his greatcoat.

Kuban Shield

Instituted: 21 September 1943
Rarity: scarce
Known maker(s)/markings: unmarked

This shield was instituted on 21 September 1943 and is similar in design to the Crimean Shield. It was also produced, like the former, in three distinct manufacturing methods and was produced from both ferrous and non ferrous metal plates, which then had a bronze wash applied. The design was stamped into the plate and had the Army eagle at the top clutching a wreath surrounding a swastika. On either side of the wreath is the date '19' and '43' respectively. There is a band just touching the bottom of the wreath with the word 'KUBAN' in block capitals. Beneath this is a zigzag broad line representing the bridgehead for which the badge was introduced. Also featuring are the locations 'KRYMSKAJA' in the middle, 'LAGUNEN' at the top and 'NOWORO-SSIJSK' at the bottom, the German names of the most significant battles fought during the campaign.

The mighty Soviet counter-offensive, following the German defeat at Stalingrad, witnessed the German forces in the south of the Soviet Union pushed helplessly back towards the Crimea Peninsula. A defensive bridgehead was formed between the Sea of Azov and the Russian naval harbour at Novorossisk and defended from February 1943 until October that year. This successful defence allowed many German units to withdraw to comparative safety in the Crimea.

Hitler recognised this defensive achievement with a proclamation of 20 September 1943:

'To commemorate the heroic battle in the Kuban bridgehead, I institute the Kuban Shield. The Kuban Shield will be worn on the left sleeve of the uniform. The Kuban Shield is awarded as a battle badge to all members of the armed forces and those under the command of the Wehrmacht who, since 1 February 1943, have been honourably engaged in the battle for the Kuban bridgehead on land, in the air or at sea. The awards will be made in my name by Generalfeldmarschall von Kleist. The recipient will also receive a certificate of possession. Implementation of the awards is through the high command of the armed forces. Führer Headquarters, 20 September 1943. (signed) *Adolf Hitler.*'

The criteria for the award were one or more of:

1. To have served in the bridgehead for 60 days;

2. To have been wounded whilst serving in the bridgehead;

3. To have been engaged in one major operation in the bridgehead.

Luftwaffe and Navy personnel were also entitled to the award, with a complicated points system being employed to qualify their personnel. In the case of the Navy, for example, a U-boat attack on a convoy of ships in the Kuban area represented six points, while being on a boat sunk by enemy action represented 60 points. One day's service represented one point.

Each recipient received five examples of the shield free of charge. Posthumous awards were granted with one shield and the award citation.

Lappland Shield

Instituted: February or March 1945
Rarity: very rare
Known maker(s)/markings: unmarked

This shield was instituted in February or March 1945 and is the last official shield to be awarded by the German High Command. It is a round-bottomed shield with a flat top. Just below the top is a bar running horizontally across the shield, breaking the edge. Round the edge of the shield is a rim. On the bar is an eagle (which in fact looks more like a chicken). The eagle does not incorporate the swastika in its design; in fact it is not employed at all on the badge. Another point of interest is that the eagle looks in different ways on various badges and I have encountered six slight variations in design and production of this badge. I have not included a breakdown of variations at this juncture, as a lot more research work is required. Beneath the bar is the word 'LAPPLAND' and beneath this is a map of the area. All the examples I have encountered are crudely cast, stamped or cut out from aluminium, tin or zinc.

Photo 124: Lappland Shield. Cast in zinc, in this example, the eagle's head faces to the right.

Photo 125: Lappland Shield. This is cut from aluminium and the eagle's head faces the left. The overall **size** of the shield is smaller than illustration 124.

Some are merely engraved crudely on to a shield-shaped blank. They have been issued without a backing cloth. Round the edges of the shield are drilled a number of small holes through which the shield could be sewn to the uniform. However, some genuine examples of the shield have been encountered with cloth backings attached. Whether the recipient did this after award or if, on very few occasions, the awarding unit had the unit's tailor attach the backing, is unclear. It was intended to reward members of the 20th Mountain Army Group, which was under the command of General Boehme, who was responsible for the award of the shield.

The 20th Gebirgs-Armee included such diverse units as 6. Gebirgs-Division, 270. Infanterie-Division, Panzer Brigade *Norwegen* and 14. Luftwaffen-Felddivision. Awards on paper were certainly made before the end of the war. Genuine pay book entries for the award are known from April 1945 but it is believed that no actual awards were issued from this time.

Following the end of hostilities, the large German forces in northern Scandinavia were left mainly to their own devices under the control of their own command structures, though these answered to the British military authorities. The Germans soon found that their captor, General Thorne, contrary to normal British practice, allowed his prisoners to wear military decorations. During this period it was decided to proceed with the issue of the Lappland Shield. These could, of course, only be produced on what amounted to a cottage industry basis. Obviously the design could not feature the swastika, as the Allies would have taken umbrage at its inclusion.

It has been suggested that the privileges allowed to the German forces in this region were given because the British authorities were seriously considering allowing certain units to defend territory against the anticipated onslaught of Soviet forces. It has been claimed that this was also considered in the Vienna region of Austria. I have one pay book issued to a Rumanian SS volunteer and he categorically states that he was never taken prisoner but was held in reserve, ready to be sent to fight the Soviets.

The criteria for the award were one or more of:

1. Six months' service in the area;

2. To have been wounded in that theatre of operations;

3. To have been engaged in a major offensive or defensive battle in that region;

4. To have won a bravery award in that area.

The precise status of this award is uncertain, as one authority has noted: 'This shield is of debatable legitimacy as a national award, as it was only authorised on a local level by the army commander and not issued until after the end of hostilities which, technically, makes even genuine pieces post-war.' However, I would point out that the shield was submitted for approval at the beginning of 1945 and received it on 1 May. Commanders in the field became the legitimate instigating force and the Third Reich did not cease until 27 May 1945, therefore awards during this period have to be considered as legitimate, albeit they may not have been given official recognition by the German Federal government.

Lorient Shield, First Type

Instituted: December 1944 (?)
Rarity: extremely rare
Known maker(s)/markings: unmarked

When the Allied forces advanced from Normandy in July–August 1944 the U-boat base at Lorient was cut off. A garrison of 26,000 men was gathered from all branches of the Wehrmacht to prevent the Allies taking possession of the town and base. There were elaborate fortifications and numerous guns and the U-boat bunkers themselves were extremely thick. The garrison of Lorient survived as a pocket of resistance until the end of the war. The surrender of Lorient, the other German bases in the Bay of Biscay area and Dunkirk in the Channel were negotiated together. Lorient capitulated on 10 May 1945, in this case to US Colonel Keating, who accepted the surrender from Oberst Borst. The garrison at Lorient produced a newspaper during their nine months' siege entitled *Kurz-Nachrichten*. An issue of this newspaper was published on 10 May and carried details of the surrender, which was to take effect at 16.00 that day.

There exists great disagreement as to the authenticity of the Lorient Shield. This will probably continue until someone can come up with incontrovertible proof, one way or another, to its introduction and award before the end of hostilities.

The shield is of thin metal with a flat top and rounded bottom. The central design is of a naked warrior with a German steel helmet on his head. In his left hand is an oval shield,

Photo 126: Lorient Shield, First Type. This shield lacks definition and has a political style eagle and swastika on the warrior shield.

Photo 127: Lorient Shield, First Type. This shield is more pronounced, noticeably the sun's rays behind the warrior while the eagle and swastika are of a military type.

with an open-winged eagle clutching a wreath and swastika in its talons impressed upon it. In his right hand is a double-edged sword. He stands astride a U-boat pen with a submarine in it and in the foreground are stylised waves. From behind the warrior emanate rays. On either side of the helmeted head is '19' and '44' respectively. Running round the bottom edge of the shield is the word 'LORIENT'. This design was reportedly submitted by

Marinebaurat Fehrenberg to the garrison commander, Admiral Henneke, who authorised the production of the shield in December 1944. It is interesting to note, however, that when approached post-war for information about the shield Admiral Henneke denied any knowledge of it. The example used is one obtained from Dr Mathias, who obtained it along with ten other examples from a French intelligence officer who picked them up in the fortress at the end of hostilities.

Christian von Jettinek has stated: 'The first type was submitted and approved and the dies were produced out of cast iron. However, the dies were of inferior quality and they broke after a short while.' This gives rise to the rarity of the first form as only a few hundred were made as opposed to the originally proposed 24,000, as stated by Dr Klietmann. The badge was produced in a local fish cannery and is purported to have been produced from various materials, the most likely being the tin plate from which the cannery produced its tins. Holes were then pierced to allow the shield to be sewn on to the uniform. It has been stated that large numbers of the shield were produced but contrariwise this has been used as an argument to prove that the badge did not exist at all because very few examples have turned up. It has also been reported that Marinebaurat Fehrenberg was commissioned by General Wilhelm Fahrmbacher to produce a design for the shield, which might seemingly explain why Admiral Henneke claimed to have no knowledge of it. However, it has also been claimed that the shields were distributed to about one man in every two in the garrison on Christmas Night 1944. That Henneke knew nothing about this 'ceremony', if it took place as stated, appears very strange. Furthermore, there is a photograph of a shield whose authenticity is in no doubt; this is said to have been awarded to a French nurse who was present in Lorient during the siege, identified as Jacqueline D.

Lefèvre and de Lagarde state that Luftwaffe personnel were meant to have received a shield with their own version of the national emblem on it. Whether any of these shields were actually produced is, of course, highly debatable given the situation the Germans were in at that time. My view is that there were only small quantities produced and this gives rise to its rarity, plus the fact that a photograph of the shield being worn so far has not yet been found but, as with the Metz Cuff title, I expect that dextrous detective work will uncover one in due course.

Lorient Shield, First Type – Variation

Rarity: extremely rare
Known maker(s)/markings: unmarked

This is a variation which is almost identical to the badge previously described but, in this case, the shield is raised to symbolise the defence from air attacks which the pocket received liberally.

Photo 128:
Lorient Shield, Second Type. This is an identity disc that has been stamped.

Lorient Shield, Second Type

Rarity: extremely rare
Known maker(s)/markings: unmarked

This is not an arm shield as such but an unused identity disc which has 'FESTUNG LORIENT 1944' stamped on it in three lines. This has been reported to be an alternative design when it was impossible to reward the troops with the shield.

One interesting comment is found in *Fakes and Frauds of The Third Reich* by Freiherr von Mollendorf:

'We have a Lorient Shield given to us by a Leutnant Kröh, formerly of the Kriegsmarine and stationed in Lorient until its surrender in May of 1945. This shield is stamped by hand onto a standard blank (unperforated) zinc German identification disc and holes were punched into it (as in the case of the much rarer 'Dunkirk' Shield) to enable it to be worn on the uniform. Herr Kröh writes us that he personally has seen a number of shields similar to the one he had but has not ever seen the nude warrior now so widely depicted. It is not impossible that the two designs existed simultaneously.'

This form has also been well researched by Richard Mundschenk, who found an example that had been sewn on the uniform of a German coastal artillery officer. This was obtained in May 1945 by Staff Sergeant Ernest Edwards, a member of the 66th US Infantry Division. His unit had been engaged in the siege of the fortress and, following the surrender, moved into the fortress and occupied the area. While souvenir hunting, Edwards discovered the discarded uniform, which was unceremoniously deposited with his other treasures in a duffel bag and subsequently shipped back to the United States, where it was stored in his foot locker and then in the attic of his Maryland home. He told Mundschenk that he had met a number of Germans wearing this form of emblem. After Edwards died, his son gave Mundschenk a number of photographs, one of which showed German prisoners going into French captivity while sporting the emblem. Mundschenk has also reported his in-depth researches into the shield from which he concluded that the two types mentioned above existed only on paper and that this battle honour was rendered only in the most readily available form of material, a standard identification 'dog tag'. Existing stocks of tags were simply stamped with the designation 'FESTUNG LORIENT'.

The three variations which Mundschenk had encountered were based on Army-type oval tags. He presumed the Kriegsmarine tags were too small in size to be used. Two were of zinc and the other aluminium. The zinc ones were engraved in large capital letters, while the aluminium type was stamped in slightly smaller letters. His findings would tie in with those of Christian von Tettinek – only a few hundred of the original shields were produced because the dies broke and the identity-disc type was then created to continue the distribution of the award. It might even have been suggested that the dog-tag type would be exchanged for the formally designed shield at a later time. This might also mean that no entry would be made in the pay book, as in the case of the Dunkirk Shield, the intention being that this would be done when the shield was awarded in the proper form.

Dunkirk Shield

Instituted: January–February 1945
Number awarded: 50 approx
Rarity: extremely rare
Known maker(s)/markings: unmarked

This award was introduced by Konteradmiral Frederich Frisius some time in January or February 1945. It is a small shield produced in thin stamped brass measuring 40mm by 34mm.

129

The bottom of the shield is rounded and the top square. The edge running all the way round is gently rolled under and there is a small hole in each top corner, and another one centrally at the bottom. These holes were to allow the badge to be attached to a hat. I have seen three examples of this shield: two had no back cloth but the other one did. So whether or not it was to have been awarded with a back cloth is a point of conjecture. The central device is the watchtower of Dunkirk with stylised waves in three lines on either side of it. To each side of the tower, in line with its top, is the date '19' and '44'. Across the top in small capitals is stamped 'DUENKIRCHEN', and round the bottom of the shield is a chain of seven unbroken links.

It is believed that there were only 50 awards of this very rare shield. There is a citation that clearly indicates that it was known as *Stoßtruppabzeichen* and that it was awarded, as this term suggests, for participation in raiding parties. Whether or not a citation was rendered with every award of the shield is unknown but an official entry was made in the pay book of each recipient to allow him to wear the shield. This entry and citation would make the award a more official decoration than some previous unofficial ones. If this shield was produced to reward members of the force who were engaged in special operations this would give rise to the very small number that were supposedly awarded out of the total garrison of 15,000. One known recipient of the award was Gefreiter Sigfried Rubusch, whose pay book was made up on 30 January 1945 and had a piece of paper stuck into the last page stamped with the Dunkirk command stamp on 18 March 1945. This gives rise to the possibility that the award was introduced as early as January 1945 and was issued to commemorate the coming to power of Hitler. It could even have been given for operations as early as October 1944 and this would account for the date '1944' appearing on the shield. Another known recipient was Stabsobergefreiter Wilhelu Tjardes who received the award on 1 May 1945.

Photo 129: Dunkirk Shield. *Christian v Tettinck*

Photo 130: Citation for the Dunkirk Shield.

Im Namen des Kommandanten
der Festung Dünkirchen
verleihe ich dem
S t a b o g e f r e i t e n
Wilhelu T j a r d e s
2 . / R o n n e l
für die Teilnahme an

zwei Stoßtruppunternehmen

in Würdigung der dabei bewiesenen Umsicht
und seines mutigen Einsatzes
das
1.u.2.
S t o ß t r u p p a b z e i c h e n

Dünkirchen, den 1. Mai   1945

Der Kommandant der Kampfgruppe
G n e i s e n a u

VERLEIHUNGSURKUNDE
NR. 1

M a j o r
DIENSTGRAD

Naval Decorations, Medals and Award Badges, 1933-45

All Third Reich decorations were inter-service, that is to say all heroism, leadership or merit was recognised by one series of awards. The Roll of Honour Clasp – Navy is the only specific decoration that was for a single branch of the military organisation. However, there was one cloth form of award that was distinctly for the Navy and this was the German Cross in Gold placed on a naval backing. One other award, the Iron Cross First Class in cloth, is most likely for flying personnel, albeit it could have been employed by U-boat personnel.

German Cross in Gold, Cloth Version – Navy Blue

Instituted: 5 June 1942
Rarity: rare

On 5 June 1942 the embroidered version of the German Cross in Gold was authorised. This badge was produced purely for field use. It is a black silk embroidered swastika, outlined in gold wire on a white silk field, bordered by a gold wire cord. This has the metal

131

132

wreath, used in the construction of the metal badge, fixed to the backing. Round the outer edge of the wreath is another circle of gold wire, from which emanate embroidered rays with white tips. The backing of the badge on to which the embroidery and metal wreath are applied is in a colour corresponding to the branch of the service. The award was worn sewn on to the right breast pocket of the uniform.

This form of the decoration was intended for combat personnel who functioned in enclosed areas, which could cause damage to the enamelled swastika. Also the size of the metal star caused a potential risk in enclosed areas of being caught on projecting parts of operational equipment.

Iron Cross First Class – Japanese Type

Instituted: unofficial
Rarity: extremely rare

An interesting variation of the Iron Cross is the Japanese-made silver variety. The cross was made from Japanese silver and it is believed that only twenty-six of these crosses were produced. The German Naval Attaché in Tokyo, Admiral Paul Wenneker, who had taken up the position on 1 April 1935 and remained until the end of the war, supplied the names of two Japanese firms of jewellers who had been com-

missioned by him previously, and they undertook the order. This had been brought about by the need to award the cross to German servicemen who found themselves stranded in the Far East where no on-hand stock of medals were available. One such instance occurred when the auxiliary cruiser *Michel* was torpedoed off Yokohama by the US submarine *Tarpon*. Obermaat Konrad Metzner rescued thirty-nine men and thereby earned the Iron Cross First Class. A presentation ceremony was held shortly after this incident at which Admiral Wenneker issued the citation documents and awarded Iron Crosses First Class to Obermaat Metzner and twenty-five other men.

Iron Cross First Class – Cloth Version

Instituted: unofficial
Rarity: extremely rare
Known maker(s)/markings: unmarked

The Iron Cross First Class – Cloth Version in hand embroidery is strictly unofficial and is usually homemade in appearance. Photographic evidence shows it to have been worn and a picture of Kapitän-zur-See Wolfgang Lüth best illustrates this. He is pictured with the Iron Cross First Class and the U-boat War Badge, both in cloth. A paratrooper, Major Dr Heinrich Neumann, medical officer with the Fallschirmjäger Sturmregiment, landed on Crete wearing both a cloth Iron Cross First Class and Parachutist's Badge. When I visited him and saw his awards, he informed me the decorations in cloth form were for daily service wear, under paratrooper smocks. They were better since metal versions of the award would get caught up or poke through tunics. He also said this

Photo 133: Kapitän-zur-See Wolfgang Lüth wearing both the 1939 Iron Cross 1st Class in cloth as well as the U-boat badge in cloth.

Photo 134: Roll of Honour Clasp – Navy.

134

cloth version could be purchased privately from the Luftwaffe-kleiderkasse, the official Luftwaffe uniform store. It is therefore possible that the equivalent Kriegsmarine establishment was the source of the naval awards.

Roll of Honour Clasp – Navy

Instituted: 13 May 1944
Number awarded: 37
Rarity: extremely rare
Known maker(s)/markings: K in a circle

On 13 May 1944 Grossadmiral Dönitz instituted the naval version of the Honour Clasp to recognise those who had been entered on 'The Honour Roll of the German Navy', which had been opened in February 1943.

The badge is produced from a single stamping but the gilt wreath is slightly larger, measuring 26mm across. The oak leaves in the gilded wreath are continuous and are made up of fifteen individual bunches of irregular design, measuring 3.5mm across. The central motif is an anchor surmounted by a swastika. In this case, the swastika is mobile and also has a fine recessed line running round the edges of the legs. The field beneath the base of the anchor and the wreath should not normally be voided. The reverse takes the negative design of the obverse, being stamped. It has four fine prongs to attach it to the Iron Cross Second Class ribbon.

It was contained in a small black oblong box, with a cream flocked base on which the badge sat, with the ends of the Iron Cross ribbon being tucked underneath the bed that produced the base. On some examples of the bed, the maker's mark for Richard Klein is encountered embossed into the corner. This is

a K in a circle with three inverted chevrons in a further circle beside the first. The lid lining was of white silk.

The recipient had already to be in the possession of the Iron Cross First and Second Class. The clasp was worn on the ribbon of the Iron Cross Second Class at the second buttonhole of the uniform. If the recipient already held an Iron Cross Second Class bar, he wore only the Roll of Honour Clasp. It has been recorded that there were thirty-seven recipients, making it an extremely rare award. However, many more were manufactured. This type of honour clasp is the hardest of the three clasps to obtain for one's collection.

Recipients of the Roll of Honour Clasp

Oberleutnant (W) Wilhelm Bitterer	11 January 1945
Oberleutnant (V) Paul Cordsmeier	9 October 1944
Kapitänleutnant August Eggers	18 November 1944
Leutnant (Ing) Waldemar Geschke	31 January 1945
Matrose Heinz Glaubrecht	8 August 1944
Matrosenobergefreiter Kurt Graf	18 November 1944
Maschinenmaat Gregor Guski	8 August 1944
Leutnant-zur-See Karl-Heinz Hansen	8 August 1944
Kapitänleutnant d.R. Günter Kayser	10 October 1943
Leutnant-zur-See Joost Kirchhoff	11 January 1945
Oberleutnant-zur-See Karl-Heinz Knauth	8 November 1943
Oblt (MA) d.R. Günter Konejung	17 October 1944
Bootsmannsmaat d.R Richard Kruse	8 November 1943
Sonderführer (Kptlt) Kurt Lerch	8 November 1943
Leutnant (Ing) Albert Moors	31 January 1945
Oberleutnant-zur-See d.R. Heinz Müller	10 January 1945
Kapitänleutnant Otto Nordt	08 November 1943
Kapitänleutnant Franz Offermanns	11 January 1945
Oberbootsmannsmaat Alois Pambuch	18 November 1944
Korvettenkapitän Ottokar Paulssen	9 October 1944
Oberfähnrich-zur-See Karl-Heinz Pettke	8 August 1944
Obersteuermann Ehrhard Preuschoff	8 August 1944
Oberleutnant (MA) d.R. Hans Rademaker	31 December 1943
Kapitänleutnant Ruprecht Rössger	18 November 1944
Matrose Paul Roth	8 August 1944
Korvettenkapitän d.R. Gustave Rübel	8 November 1943
Oberfeldwebel Heinrich Schiebel	8 August 1944
Steuermannsmaat Ernst Schröger	8 August 1944
Oberleutnant-zur-See d.R. Ulrich Schütz	11 January 1945
Oberleutnant (Ing) Paul Schwarz	28 June 1943
Oberleutnant-zur-See Günther Wegener	9 October 1944
Oberwaffenwart (Spr) Friedrich Weilkes	11 January 1945
Bootsmannsmaat Günther Weiss	8 November 1943
Obermech Maat (Spr) Herbert Wilhelm	11 January 1945
Oberleutnant-zur-See Karl Konrad Winzer	8 August 1944
Sonderführer (Obersteuermann) Alfred Wolf	11 January 1945
Oberleutnant-zur-See d.R. Emil Wolf	6 September 1944

Naval War Badges 1939-45

U-boat War Badge

Instituted: 13 October 1939
Rarity: scarce
Known maker(s)/markings: unmarked,
Schwerin, G.W.L, R.K.W. (within a circle),
R.S. (both angular and round forms of the
letters), L/13, L/18, L/21, L/52, L/53

Hitler reinstituted the U-boat War Badge on 13 October 1939. The badge was similar to that of the 1914–18 issue, except that the Third Reich emblem of the eagle and swastika replaced the imperial crown, with the U-boat being modified to a more modern type. The badge is oval in the form of a wreath of laurel leaves with a cross ribbon tie at the base. On either side are seven bunches of three leaves. The inner and outer edges of the wreath do not take the outline of the leaves. At the apex is an open-winged eagle whose wings run between the two arms of the laurel bunches. The wings have four lines of fletch on each side while the body of the eagle has a small chest surmounted by a small head facing to the viewer's left. It clutches a small swastika in its talons. This can have the fields between the arms either voided or solid. Across the lower part of the badge is a submarine facing to the viewer's left. The badge measures 48mm across and is 39mm high from the base of the wreath to the top of the eagle's head. The wingspan is 31.5mm and the swastika measures 7.5mm across the tips. The reverse is flat and on the back of the submarine in this type is usually found the maker's mark of Schwerin und Sohn of Berlin 68. Also on this type is a broad pin, with laid-down hinge at the top and large hook at the bottom. Paul Caseberg of Berlin designed the badge.

Photo 135: U-boat War Badge.

Photo 136: Reverse of U-boat War Badge showing how the badge has been customised to fit the uniforms better.

The construction of the badge varied due to war conditions. The best examples of these badges are commonly referred to as being tombac or brass and are manufactured from a copper-based alloy. Tombac badges are early war period, 1939–42. Being struck in brass, a very fine detail is given to the badge, which is normally found with segmented arms to the swastika. You can always identify a Zimmermann-made award, as all four arms of the swastika are segmented. In the case of Mayer and Schickle badges only three arms are cut out; the top arm remains solid.

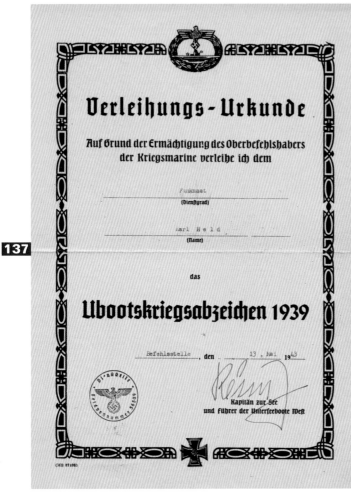

Photo 137: Citation for the U-boat War Badge.

Photo 138: U-boat War Badge in cloth.

Photo 139: The death citation for a lost U-boat serviceman. This is prior to the citation illustration 137.

Zinc or pot metal badges are late war period, 1942–5. It is believed that the switch from tombac/brass to zinc occurred sometime towards the end of 1942 following the introduction of metal conservation regulations. This is also supported by the fact that the original S-boat War Badge, Second Type, which was instituted in January 1943, is to be found only in zinc. The poorer quality badges were produced in zinc or pot metal with a needle pin, again with the maker's mark being stamped on to the reverse. The pot metal, which was gilded, quite often deteriorates to give a rather unpleasant appearance.

Admiral Raeder announced the introduction of the badge on 13 October 1939: 'I hereby order the institution of the Submarine War Badge for crew members of submarines in the Navy. The commanders of the submarines will present the badges. The badge can be presented to all officers, NCOs and crew members who serve on submarines directed against the enemy and who prove themselves.'

The criteria for the award were one or more of:

Für Führer, Volk und Vaterland gab sein Leben

am 31.10.43

der Funkmaat

Karl Held

Im Auftrage des Oberbefehlshabers der Kriegsmarine ist darüber diese Urkunde ausgestellt worden.

Im Westen, den 31. Oktober 1943

Kap. z. See und ... der U-Boote West
Dienstgrad, Dienststellung

1. To have been involved in a particularly successful mission;

2. To have completed or participated in more than three missions;

3. To have won a bravery decoration in a mission, even if it was the man's first;

4. To have been wounded on a mission, again even if it was the first mission or wound.

The badge with citation was also rendered to the next of kin of those lost at sea in a U-boat due to enemy action.

The badge was to be worn on the service jacket, blue and white jacket, blue and white mess jacket, pullover and blue and white shirt, on the left side like the World War 1 Submarine Badge. It was to be worn during duty and off-duty hours.

The badge was presented in a variety of ways. The brass high-grade badges were

Photo 140: U-boat War Badge Miniature.

Photo 141: Reverse of U-boat War Badge Miniature.

usually awarded in a black, hinged box, with a black or blue velvet base, with a white silk lid lining. The poorer quality badges were awarded in paper packets. These are quite rare as they were seldom saved after the award ceremony.

There was provision for a cloth type of the badge and this came in two versions. Those for enlisted men and NCOs are gold cotton on a blue felt backing. The type for officers was woven in Bevo style in gilt wire, on a blue silk oval backing. Both of these forms could be sewn on to naval uniforms but from the lack of photographs of them in wear, it seems they must have been very unpopular. The officers' version of the U-boat Badge was not bullion embroidered. Perhaps a few one-off examples may exist in gold bullion, worked onto a felt padded badge, but these would be purely private-purchase items.

U-boat War Badge – Variations

Rarity: scarce
Known maker(s)/markings: F.O.

There are three or four slight variations in the production of the U-boat War Badge but I have, for convenience, condensed them to two. The first version already described is normally known as the Schwerin type. The first variant has three main characteristics separating it from its Schwerin counterpart. The first is in the design of the eagle's chest, which has a pronounced heart, or shield, shape sur-

90

Photo 142: U-boat War Badge – variation of the swastika has had the arms rounded.

Photo 143: Reverse of the U-boat War Badge showing the maker's mark: 'F O' – Friedrich Orth/Wien.

Photo 144: U-boat War Badge – French Type.

Photo 145: Reverse of the U-boat War Badge – French Type showing the typical pin hook construction.

U-boat War Badge – French Type

Rarity: rare
Known maker(s)/markings: unmarked – Mourgeon (Paris), Bacqueville

The second type I have categorised by its French manufacture. The obverse has a design very similar to the normal U-boat badge. The reverse has a French-style pin, hinge and hook. The hinge is of two parallel pieces of thin metal that have semi-circular outer ends, while the inner ones are flat and held apart by a small vertical piece that doubles up and acts as a rest for the pin. The two parallel pieces of metal are drilled and have a large-headed brass pin placed through them to act as a pivot for the pin. The pin is a flat-bellied one that tapers to the point. The hook is of the C form soldered directly to the reverse of the badge. The pin, hook and hinge are placed on the badge in a horizontal configuration and at the top is placed a hook designed to fit through a loop sewn on to the tunic that holds the badge securely to the uniform.

There has been controversy about the status of these badges. It is without doubt that they were produced in the war period but if they were ever awarded is still uncertain. The range consists of the entire awards bar, Mine-Sweepers, Sub-Chasers and Escort Vessels War Badge, Blockade Runners and those awards

mounted by bold symmetrical fletching. The second point to notice is that the laurel leaves which produce the wreath are more pronounced, the tips of those laurel leaves giving the impression of being worn. The central vein of each leaf is also more pronounced. The third area of difference is in the submarine where there are variations in the deck gun, flag, conning tower and water line. Some of the finer quality badges have a segmented swastika but these are quite rare.

The reverse is plain with a horizontal hinge, hook and pin. The hinge is a rolled form of barrel and soldered directly on to the badge at the viewer's right. The needle pin is held to the hinge with the shepherd's crook form of attachment. The hook is of the C type soldered directly to the reverse of the badge. The maker's mark is found in raised capital letters, F.O. for Frederick Orth. The badge measures 48.7mm across and is 39.6mm from the base to the top of the eagle's head.

introduced after 1943. I have also seen a document purporting to be from a family member of a French Navy officer who worked in the French Navy Ministry in Paris after the war. He allegedly found a stock of these badges in the ministry building and traded them to American servicemen in return for goods, which were in short supply in France at the time.

U-boat War Badge with Diamonds

Number awarded: 1
Rarity: unique
Known maker(s)/markings: C.S.U.C.
BERLIN 68

Admiral Raeder instructed the firm of Schwerin of Berlin to produce a special grade of the U-boat badge that was to be a once-only award to be rendered to Admiral Dönitz to recognise the successes Dönitz had achieved in U-boat warfare. This beautiful badge was struck in solid gold, proofed to the gold standard of .535, and was set with a total of twenty-one diamonds. This included nine rose-cut diamonds set in the swastika, and twelve larger stones implanted and surmounted upon the laurel wreath that formed the outside of the badge. The basic design and dimensions were the same as for the U-boat War Badge. The quality of the badge was exceptional. On the reverse of the badge was the maker's mark or logo, C.S.U.C. BERLIN 68. This logo was produced in two lines. The badge had a wide flat pin on the reverse, the

Photo 146: U-boat War Badge with Diamonds. A one-time award to GrandAdmiral Karl Dönitz.

Photo 147: GrandAdmiral Karl Dönitz. His special War Badge with Diamonds and his World War 2 U-boat badge can clearly be seen.

hinge at the top was of the laid-down box type, and it had a massive hook at the other end. Dönitz wore this badge in conjunction with his World War 1 badge and continued to wear it right up to his surrender in May 1945. Unfortunately for the numismatic world, at the end of the war the badge was removed from Dönitz and crudely de-Nazified by having the swastika torn off.

Dönitz later indicated that the badge was awarded without a citation and the box was just a plain black box with a ramp for the badge to sit on at the base.

U-boat War Badge with Diamonds – Types A & B

Number awarded: 28
Rarity: extremely rare
Known maker(s)/markings: Schwerin

A special U-boat badge was produced to be awarded to particularly successful commanders. This prestigious award was not a government or Reich award but one, which was purely from the commander of the Navy. This badge followed the design of the standard award but had a separate swastika set with nine brilliants, which was placed on the swastika incorporated into the design of the badge. The size of this swastika varied, creating what have been called the A and B Types. The A Type represents the badge as first awarded; the B Type was issued some time in late 1942. The precise date of the change and the reasons for it are unclear. Schwerin of Berlin produced both types.

The A Type badge was produced in tombac, which was either gold-plated or fire-gilded. In this type the second swastika is placed so that its top point rests on the lower chest of the eagle and the bottom point is positioned on top of the

Photo 148: U-boat War Badge with Diamonds – Type-A.

Photo 149: Reverse of U-boat War Badge with Diamonds – Type-A.

conning tower of a Type VII U-boat. This swastika is finely handcrafted from solid silver with burnished edges and a raised beaded border to the arms. The field produced has nine

Photo 150: U-boat War Badge with Diamonds – Type-B.

Photo 151: Reverse of U-boat War Badge with Diamonds – Type-B.

individual grounds, each being bordered by a raised line in the form of a square, into which is set a rose-cut simulated stone or white sapphire, held by four claws, one in each corner. The swastika is 13mm in diameter and 2mm thick. The badge measures 48mm wide and 38.5mm high from the base of the wreath to the top of the eagle's head and is 3mm thick.

The reverse shows clearly the swastika applied over the cut-out swastika of the badge. Holes are drilled to allow the light to pass through, thus enhancing the fire of the brilliants; these are reamed out to maximise the effect. The reverse is matt finished. The badge itself is flat with a large pin and hinge construction and a C-form hook soldered directly to the bottom of the badge. The maker's name, in indented letters, is on the reverse of the U-boat in two lines, 'SCHWERIN, BERLIN 68'. On the two examples of this type I have examined, a claw line is visible on either side.

The B Type badge is, to all intents and purposes, the same as the A Type badge but is struck in unmarked solid silver that is fire-gilded. The swastika is applied to the badge in the same manner and is formed in the same way but has a diameter of 8.5mm and is inset with nine small rose-cut diamonds. The badge has similar measurements and reverse to the A Type badge.

The badge was rendered in a protective black or exceptionally dark blue box, which is hinged with a press-stud holder. The base of the box has a raised plinth on which the badge sits. Through this plinth is a slit to take the pin. In the case of the Schwerin badge that I examined, the lining was of a very dark blue but it was black velvet in the case of the Foerster & Barth variation of the badge (see below). The lid liner in both was of white satin but neither had the maker's name or logo stencilled on to it.

The known recipient of the A Type badge was Kapitän Viktor Schutze, commander of *U-103* and commander of the U-boat School, who was awarded the Knight's Cross of the Iron Cross on 11 December 1940 for actions in the North Sea. He received the Oak Leaves on 14 July 1941.

Known recipients of the B Type badge were:

Kapitän Klaus Scholtz, commander of *U-108*, who was awarded the Knight's Cross of the Iron Cross on 26 December 1941 and received the Oak Leaves on 10 September 1942 for operations in the Atlantic.

Kapitän Carl Emmermann, commander of *U-172* and commander of the 31st Submarine Flotilla, who was awarded the Knight's Cross of the Iron Cross on 27 November 1942. He received the Oak Leaves on 4 July 1943 for continued successful sorties in the Atlantic.

Kapitänleutnant Georg Lassen, commander of *U-160*, who was awarded the Knight's Cross of the Iron Cross on 10 August 1942 and received the Oak Leaves on 7 March 1943. Raeder personally handed the award to him in 1943 and there was no case or document accompanying it.

From these known awards and the dates of the bestowal of the Oak Leaves, it is fairly safe to deduce the theory of the A and B Types as well as the period of change. However, Klaus Scholtz had a second piece and that had a large swastika similar to the A Type but with the noticeable differences that the swastika did not have the beaded edge or the square settings for the stones which, in this case, were white sapphires. The settings were not drilled through to the reverse and the badge itself is believed to have been struck from tombac.

To have qualified for the badge the recipient had to be a holder of the Knight's Cross of the Iron Cross with Oak Leaves. The twenty-eight officers who qualified and received this award are listed below.

Korvettenkapitän Heinrich Bleichrodt	commander *U-48, U-109*
Fregattenkapitän Albrecht Brandi	commander *U-617, U-967*
Korvettenkapitän Otto von Bulow	commander *U-404*
Korvettenkapitän Carl Emmermann	commander *U-172*
Kapitänleutnant Engelbert Endrass	commander *U-46, U-567*
Kapitänleutnant Freidrich Guggenberger	commander *U-81*
Korvettenkapitän Robert Gysae	commander *U-98, U-177*
Korvettenkapitän Reinhard Hardegen	commander *U-123*
Kapitän-zur-See Werner Hartmann	commander *U-37, U-198*
Korvettenkapitän Werner Henke	commander *U-515*
Fregattenkapitän Otto Kretschmer	commander *U-99*
Kapitänleutnant Hans-Gunther Lange	commander *U-711*
Korvettenkapitän Georg Lassen	commander *U-160*
Fregattenkapitän Heinrich Lehman-Willenbrock	commander *U-96*
Fregattenkapitän Heinrich Liebe	commander *U-38*
Kapitän-zur-See Wolfgang Lüth	commander *U-138, U-181*
Kapitän-zur-See Karl-Freidrich Merten	commander *U-68*
Korvettenkapitän Johann Mohr	commander *U-124*
Kapitänleutnant Rolf Mützelburg	commander *U-203*
Korvettenkapitän Günther Prien	commander *U-47*
Kapitänleutnant Joachim Schepke	commander *U-100*
Korvettenkapitän Adalbert Schnee	commander *U-201*
Kapitän-zur-See Klaus Scholtz	commander *U-108*
Korvettenkapitän Herbert Schultze	commander *U-48*
Kapitän-zur-See Victor Schutze	commander *U-103*
Fregattenkapitän Reinhard Suhren	commander *U-564*
Kapitänleutnant Rolf Thomsen	commander *U-1202*
Fregattenkapitän Erich Topp	commander *U-552*

It has been reported that Reichsmarschall Göring received a badge in acknowledgement of his award to Grossadmiral Dönitz of the Combined Pilot's Badge with Diamonds. Whether or not a formal bestowal of the U-boat Badge with Diamonds followed this occurrence is unknown. Various stories are told of the meetings between the two. It seems certain that Dönitz was awarded the Pilot's Badge but it is less likely that Göring received the Submarine Badge with Diamonds from Dönitz. Dönitz would have made the award begrudgingly, as it contravened his intended award criteria for this badge. In correspondence with the author, Dönitz also stated he had no recollection of receiving the Combined Pilot's Badge with Diamonds or the German Order, which Hitler had also supposedly awarded him.

U-boat War Badge with Diamonds – Variation

Rarity: extremely rare
Known maker(s)/markings: L/21

There is another version of this award badge. The wreath is a finer type. The eagle has a heart-shaped chest with broad fletching and its legs are separated to hold the swastika. This is set with nine rose-cut diamonds, which are set directly into the arms of the swastika. The reverse is semi-hollow with a thin square pin, which has the silver content .800 stamped into it and the maker's mark L/21. In the example that has been examined, this is in a square,

which has been double-struck. This badge is of particularly high quality and was produced by the firm of Foerster & Barth. Few of these badges are known to exist and whether or not they were awarded, or produced by that firm as prototypes, is unknown.

U-boat Combat Clasp – Bronze, Silver Class

Instituted: 15 May 1944 and 24 November 1944
Rarity: rare, very rare
Known maker(s)/markings:
Ausf./Schwerin/Berlin 68

On 15 May 1944 Admiral Dönitz introduced the U-boat Combat Clasp in Bronze. This was done to follow, and come in line with, the Army and the Luftwaffe. It was to commemorate and recognise the particular courage required in the U-boat service.

The original enabling order states:

1. In recognition of the continual tough actions of the U-boats and their brave, tenacious and exemplary battles, I institute the U-boat Combat Clasp in Bronze.

2. The award is conditional on general merit and fulfilment of requirements.

3. The requirements for the award of the U-boat Combat Clasp in Bronze shall be separately established.

54

55

4. The U-boat Combat Clasp will be awarded through the flotilla commanders on my authority.

5. The clasp will be worn immediately above the ribbon bar.

On 24 November 1944, a silver grade was introduced for further acts of valour and a gold version of the badge was produced. There was no authorisation for the gold class but it may, in due course, come to light. No examples of the gold award are known.

The exact details of the criteria for the award of either of these badges are uncertain and when I corresponded with Admiral Dönitz about the matter, he replied that they were 'to be something of the greatest bravery'. Awards were made by recommendations from the

Photo 152: U-boat War Badge with Diamonds – Variation.

Photo 153: Reverse of U-boat War Badge with Diamonds – Variation.

Photo 154: U-boat Combat Clasp – Bronze.

Photo 155: Reverse of U-boat Combat Clasp – Bronze.

Photo 156: Reverse of U-boat Combat Clasp – Silver.

Photo 157: U-boat Combat Clasp – Silver.

156

157

U-boat commanders. They were to take into account the number of trips the proposed recipient had undertaken and the danger encountered in each sortie. The personal bravery of any crewmember was also taken into account. In effect therefore the criteria could vary with each U-boat engagement. Actual award was not made until each recommendation had received personal approval from Grossadmiral Dönitz. The clasp was to be considered as having equivalent value to the War Merit Cross First Class with Swords. It was worn on the upper left breast above the ribbon bar.

The maker and original designer of the badge was Peekhaus and the logo is found on the reverse of the badge in raised capital letters on either side of the central wreath. These two badges are identical except for the colour applied to them. In the case of the bronze badge, the colour is applied to the badge and then artificially patinated. The silver badge has a form of silver plating that is then frosted, with the highlights gently polished. The silver plating often lessens the clarity of the design of this badge, filling the fine die striking and diminishing the crispness of its lines.

There are two types of production method and design used in the construction of this badge, which can be encountered in both grades. Shortly after production had begun the badge was manufactured in die-cast rather than die-struck zinc. The exact date of change is unknown but was probably in December 1944 or January 1945. This can be concluded because the silver grade, introduced in November 1944, is also encountered in the first pattern. The change in manufacturing technique was most likely made on economic grounds. It economised on the time required to assemble the clasp as well as materials, allowing the hinge block to be cast integrally with the badge. Although the second pattern is die-cast, the badges would be trimmed on a finishing die and usually still show the shear marks around the edges, which are associated with die striking.

The obverse of the first and second form is identical in every respect. The badge is in the form of a small U-boat measuring 30mm by 24mm, with an eagle with downswept wings at the top of the surrounding laurel wreath. The wings of the eagle follow the line of the wreath. Crossed swords, indicating the combat

status of the decoration, replace the ribbon ties at the base of the wreath. These are broad-bladed with a double edge and central fuller. The handles have four lines making up the grip, round pommels and broad straight quillons. On either side of the swords, which rest on an unadorned field, are five bunches of three laurel leaves. The inner and outer edges of the wreath formed by them do not follow their line but are solid and symmetrical. The central badge is flanked on either side by three rows of oak leaves with two leaves in each row. The upper and lower rows have smaller oak leaves. The length of the badge is 76.5mm and the width of the leaves is 15mm. The badge is gently bowed along its length to allow for a comfortable fit to the chest.

The difference between the forms lies in the design of the reverse. Immediately behind the central motif the first pattern has an oval recessed area. It has a brass flat pin, wide at the centre and tapering towards each end. The hook is made from a flat brass strip. The hook is also in brass. Both were separate pieces soldered to the reverse. To the left-hand reverse was added the relief inscription 'ENTW/PEEKHAUS/BERLIN' and to the right 'AUSF/SCHWERIN/BERLIN SW68.' In the case of the second pattern, the reverse is perfectly flat in the centre and has the wording slightly altered to read 'ENTWURF/PEEKHAUS' on the left, and 'AUS./SCHWERIN/BERLIN 68' on the right. It has an integral hinge and a C-form hook recessed into the body of the badge, with a circular mark that is then moulded up to the stem of the C. The pin is large and goes horizontally across the badge from right to left. The structure of the pin is usually fluted. It is important to note that small details such as the use of a full stop after the abbreviation 'AUSF' on the second pattern are not present on the first pattern.

It was awarded in a plain paper packet with the name of the badge printed on the front. The silver class was sometimes awarded in an oblong blue card box, with a blue flock lining.

Photo 158: Reverse of U-boat Combat Clasp – Silver. This shows the first type of construction.

Photo 159: Destroyer War Badge.

Photo 160: Reverse of the Destroyer War Badge. This has a long pin, probably due to the pin not being clipped in the finishing process. It also shows the marker's mark on the pin four in a box.

159

Destroyer War Badge

Instituted: 4 June 1940
Rarity: scarce
Known maker(s)/markings: unmarked, 4, 4 (in square), 14, FO, JFS, Schwerin, S.H.u.Co., WII, R.S. (both angular and round forms of the letters), L/18, L/21, L/53

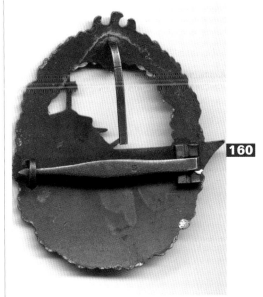

160

The badge is an oval wreath of oak leaves with a crossed ribbon tie at the base. The arms of the wreath meet at the apex with a small closed-winged eagle positioned between them. The wreath has two leaves emanating horizontally, one from each side of the ties. Above each horizontal leaf is the tip of a single leaf and from this formation, on either side, are six bunches of two leaves irregularly positioned and crowned by a single leaf that touches the outer edge of the eagle's wing. The outer edge of the wreath takes the line of the jagged edges of the individual leaves.

A destroyer comes through the wreath with its superstructure joining the inner edge of the right-hand side of the wreath and its prow breaking the left-hand side. Beneath the prow is a large bow wake, indicating that the destroyer is travelling at high speed in a heavy sea. The wreath is gilded and the ship and sea are oxidised dark black silver, with some of the highlights being brightly polished. The badge measures 54mm from the base to the top of the eagle's head and 45mm across the badge from the tip of the prow to the opposite side of the wreath. The wreath itself is 7mm wide.

The reverse is plain and slightly concave. This badge can have a variety of hinges and hooks. When the pin construction is horizontal, there is usually a small hook positioned behind the eagle's body at the top of the badge. This is employed to hook through a small cotton eyelet on the tunic to maintain the badge in an upright and secure position. The reverse is blackened and the maker's name can be encountered in raised capital letters, as can the logo of the individual firm.

The designer of the badge was Paul Caseberg of Berlin and it was first produced in bronze and then later, due to war constraints, in zinc or pot metal. A cloth version was authorised for wear on the dark blue uniform. For this the badge was produced in all gold thread on dark blue wool.

Photo 161: Destroyer War Badge by Schwerin.

Photo 162: Reverse of the Destroyer War Badge. This shows the marker's name Schwerin, Berlin 68.

Photo 163: Destroyer War Badge Miniature.

Photo 164: Destroyer War Badge in bullion for officer ranks.

Photo 165: Destroyer War Badge in cloth.

Grossadmiral Raeder introduced this badge on 4 June 1940, during the battle of Narvik. This badge was initially to reward the crews under the command of Kommodore Bonte involved in the battle. It was awarded in conjunction with the Narvik Shield, but was a separate distinction from the Shield. In an order dated 22 October 1940, award and authorisation for the wear of the badge was extended to crewmembers of other destroyers, or vessels that could be described as such including torpedo boats and Schnellboote (literally 'fast boats' – abbreviated to S-boats – or, as these last were known to the Allies, E-boats). Following the initial awards for participation in the battle of Narvik the criteria for the award were one or more of:

1. To have been wounded;

2. To have served on a ship sunk by enemy action;

3. To have participated in three separate engagements with the enemy;

4. To have completed twelve operational sorties without enemy action;

5. To have performed an heroic action for which no other decoration had been awarded.

The badge was worn on the lower left breast of the naval uniform, underneath the Iron Cross First Class or similar award.

In the early days of the war it was presented in a blue box with blue velvet base and white silk lid lining and, later, in a plain paper packet which can be found in the usual three or four colours, with the name of the badge printed in black on the front.

Photo 166:
Destroyer War Badge
– French Type.

Photo 167: Reverse
of the Destroyer War
Badge – French Type.
This shows the
typical pin link and
hook of the
Bacqueville-made
badges.

Photo 168:
Destroyer War Badge
with Diamonds.

Photo 169: Reverse
of the Destroyer War
Badge with
Diamonds.

Destroyer War Badge – French Type

Rarity: rare
Known maker(s)/markings: unmarked –
Mourgeon (Paris), Bacqueville

This badge was produced in France and is very
similar in design to its previously described
German counterpart, with the notable exception that the wreath in the badge is made up
of oak leaves, as is the case for other badges of
this type of French production. In this version
the destroyer is more finely worked and the
detail is greatly enhanced. The eagle surmounting the badge is identical to the original
version. The badge measures 54mm from the
base to the tip of the eagle's head and 44.5mm
from the tip of the prow to the outside of the

wreath, while the wreath measures 8mm at its widest point.

The reverse has a French-style pin, hinge and hook. The hinge is of two parallel pieces of thin metal with a semi-circular outer end, while the inner ends are flat and held apart by a small vertical piece that doubles up and acts as a rest for the pin. The two parallel pieces of metal are drilled and have a large-headed brass pin placed through them to act as a pivot for the pin. The pin is flat-bellied and tapers to the point. The hook is of the C-form, soldered directly to the reverse of the badge. The pin, hook and hinge are placed on the badge in a horizontal configuration and at the top is placed a hook to fit through a loop sewn on to the tunic and hold the badge securely to the uniform. The reverse of the badge is slightly concave and smooth and has a black oxidised finish over the pin assembly. Whereas in a number of other French-made versions of German naval awards the negative imprint of the obverse is found in the reverse, it is not noticed on this type.

The container in which these badges were given is a buff box, with a separate bottom and lid with the corners stapled together. The badge inside is found wrapped in tissue paper.

Destroyer War Badge with Diamonds

Rarity: unique
Known maker(s)/markings: .08990

This version of the Destroyer War Badge is set with nine small rose-cut diamonds. These diamonds are placed into a swastika, which is clutched in the talons of the eagle. The swastika is larger than that found on the normal badge; this is similar to the other badges set with diamonds. It is struck in solid silver and carries the .800 fine silver mark on the reverse. The pin is horizontal with a hook and heavy hinge. Presumably this badge was intended to recognise particularly successful destroyer captains who had won the Oak Leaves to the Knight's Cross. However, none of these badges is known to have been awarded. One theory is that this was the badge that was going to be awarded to successful S-boat commanders,

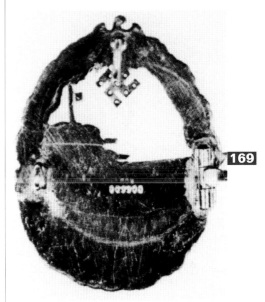

who were entitled to the Destroyer War Badge after 22 October 1940, but that this badge was superseded by the introduction of the S-boat Badge with Diamonds. That was, however, awarded later in the war and will be described below.

170

Photo 170: Mine-Sweeper, Sub-Chaser and Escort Vessel War Badge.

Photo 171: Reverse of the Mine-Sweeper, Sub-Chaser and Escort Vessel War Badge showing vertical pin.

Photo 172: Reverse of the Mine-Sweeper, Sub-Chaser and Escort Vessel War Badge showing horizontal pin.

Photo 173: Mine-Sweeper, Sub-Chaser and Escort Vessel War Badge – miniature stick pin.

Mine-Sweeper, Sub-Chaser and Escort Vessel War Badge

Instituted: 31 August 1940
Rarity: common
Known maker(s)/markings: unmarked, A, AS, AS (in triangle), R.K., Schwerin, W (in a circle), WH, R.S. & S., R.S. (both angular and round forms of the letters), L/18, L/21

This badge takes the form of a chemically blued silver waterspout rising from the waves of the sea, with the outer edge being formed by a wreath of laurel leaves. The inner and outer edges of the wreath take the line of the leaves which form it. The bottom has a tie formed in three raised lines, with four acorns, positioned one at each corner. From the tie emanate seven bunches of two oak leaves which are positioned irregularly to form the wreath, with a single oak leaf at the apex. Each junction of bunches is punctuated by a pair of acorns, one on either side of the wreath. A broad-winged eagle clutching a swastika in its claws surmounts this. The badge measures 54mm from the base to the top of the eagle's head. The width of the badge is 43.5mm and the width of the wreath is 7.5mm. The eagle's wingspan is 28mm. Another version of this badge has measurements of 56mm, 45mm, 8mm and 30mm.

On the reverse is a large pin, which is usually vertical, but is also encountered in the horizontal position. The horizontal form has a

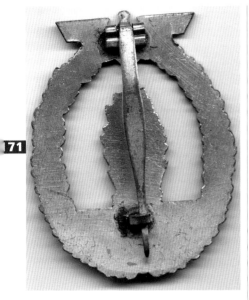

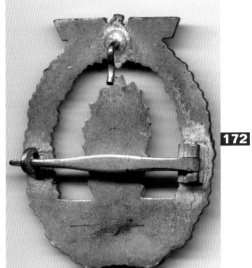

hook behind the eagle, which helped to fix the badge to the uniform through a small cotton stitch. This had the double effect of keeping the badge flat to the tunic at the top and should the pin have become open and free from the tunic, the badge hung from this cotton loop. Usually these horizontal pins are of the thin needle type. Most badges carry the maker's logo or address on the reverse and are finished with silver backing, but others, usually of a later production, are gilded.

It was worn on the left breast of the service tunic, underneath the Iron Cross First Class or equivalent grade of award.

The quality of these badges varies. The highest quality badges are formed of brass, finely detailed with a segmented swastika, the wreath being finely gilded and the waterspout, and in some examples the waves, being silver-plated, the waves being then chemically blued or blackened. The lesser quality examples are of zinc, pot or monkey metal, which were poorly struck with a very inferior finish.

A cloth version was authorised for wear on the dark blue uniform. In it the wreath is exe-cuted in yellow cotton and the waterspout and sea in silver cotton thread, all on a blue backing.

The award container varies widely to include a blue box with navy blue flocking base and silk lid liner, through to the paper packet,

which comes in various colours, with the name of the badge printed on its front in black.

Grossadmiral Raeder directed Otto Placzek to create this special badge for mine-sweepers. The badge was instituted on 31 August 1940 for officers and ratings of the German Navy and the civilian Merchant Marine employed in its service. The first award of this badge was made on 28 November 1940.

The criteria for the award were one or more of:

1. Completion of three operational sorties;

2. Being wounded during an operational sortie;

3. If the ship had been sunk by enemy action;

4. Exemplary conduct over a six-month period;

5. The completion of a specially dangerous mission in a mined area;

6. A mission of 25 days or more on escort duty.

Photo 174: Mine-Sweeper, Sub-Chaser and Escort Vessel War Badge in cloth.

Photo 175: Schnellboot War Badge – First Type.

Photo 176: Reverse of the Schnellboot War Badge – First Type. This shows the maker's name: Schwerin, Berlin 68.

Photo 177: Schnellboot War Badge – First Type. This badge produced in zinc is lacking in quality of that illustrated in 175

Photo 178: Reverse of the Schnellboot War Badge – First Type. This body produced with zinc shows the vertical pin and 'O' mark.

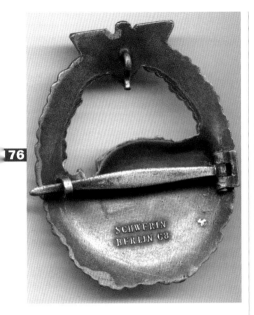

Mine-Sweeper, Sub-Chaser and Escort Vessel War Badge with Diamonds

Number awarded: 1 (?)
Rarity: extremely rare
Known maker(s)/markings: Unknown

This badge was identical in most respects to the standard badge. It was, however, produced in silver and a second swastika was superimposed on the first. This second swastika is in a diagonal box form and has nine rose cut diamonds set into it. One example has been traced as being awarded.

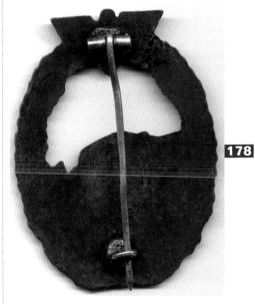

Schnellboot War Badge – First Type

Instituted: 30 May 1941
Rarity: very rare
Known maker(s)/markings: Schwerin, Ausf. Schwerin Berlin 68 in conjunction with Peekhaus designer's mark

Originally, qualifying S-boat men wore the Destroyer Badge but later there were three Schnellboot badges. This First Type badge was designed by Wilhelm Ernst Peekhaus of Berlin and was instituted on 30 May 1941. The design of the badge consists of an oak-leaf wreath, which has a tie at the base, and surmounting it at the top an eagle clutching a swastika. The wings on this eagle are stubby. The tie has a broad raised central spine with a

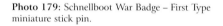

Photo 179: Schnellboot War Badge – First Type miniature stick pin.

Photo 180: Schnellboot War Badge – Second Type miniature stick.

Photo 181: Schnellboot War Badge – First Type miniature stick pin reverse.

small raised edge line on either side. From this emanate seven bunches of two oak leaves positioned in irregular order with a single acorn being positioned haphazardly at the junction of the leaves. Both the wreath and eagle are finely gilded. The badge measures 57mm from the base to the top of the eagle's head and 45mm across the badge. The wreath measures 7.5mm and the eagle's wingspan is 23.5mm, the height of the eagle and swastika being 14mm.

The main subject of the badge is an S-boat ploughing through the sea. This is an S-30 Class vessel. You can clearly see there is an upsweep over the torpedo tube loading doors and the portholes; the *S-30* Class alone had this combination of features. The boat comes only halfway through the wreath and is finished in silver. The sea is blue-black with the crests of the waves being burnished silver.

The reverse of the badge in the most desirable examples has a scalloped effect on the reverse of the S-boat and the reverse of the wreath is flat. On this form of manufacture the manufacturer's name and address is found in two lines, in small raised letters 'SCHWERIN/BERLIN 68'. It usually has a horizontal pin. When this is the case, a small hook can be found which helped to secure the badge to the uniform. It also can be found with a vertical pin construction and in this case the reverse of the badge is normally flat. Also, in rarer examples, the maker's address or logo can be found. The badge was worn on the left breast pocket, beneath the Iron Cross First Class or like award.

The badge was usually presented in a blue box with a blue flock base, with white silk lid liner and the badge title stencilled in silver on the outer upper lid of the box. This badge was discontinued soon after its inception and therefore it is considered very rare.

The criteria for the award were one or more of:

1. Twelve sorties against enemy vessels or installations;

2. Outstanding leadership;

3. A particularly successful mission;

4. To have been wounded in the course of an action, even if this was the first

182

183

Photo 182: Schnellboot War Badge – Second Type.

Photo 183: Reverse of the Schnellboot War Badge – Second Type. This shows the horizontal pins and the marker's mark as intertwined in a triangle.

Schnellboot War Badge – Second Type

Instituted: January 1943
Rarity: scarce
Known maker(s)/markings: unmarked, L/18, AS, AS (in a triangle), R.K., R.S. (both angular and round forms of the letters), Schwerin, Ausf. Schwerin Berlin 68 in conjunction with Peekhaus designer's mark

Why was the pattern changed? (Such a change is unusual and in fact I cannot think of another qualification or combat badge other than pre-war Pilot–Observer or Aircrew Badge that took such a radical change.) The reason

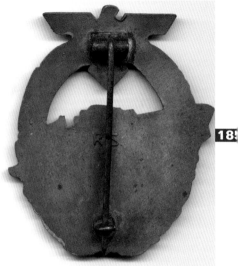

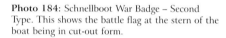

Photo 184: Schnellboot War Badge – Second Type. This shows the battle flag at the stern of the boat being in cut-out form.

Photo 185: Schnellboot War Badge – Second Type. This shows the vertical pin and the marker's mark, RS – Rudolf Souval.

Photo 186: Schnellboot War Badge – French Type.

Photo 187: Reverse of the Schnellboot War Badge – French Type. This shows the typical pin hinge and hook of the Bacqueville-made badges.

was that a new model Schnellboot was introduced to supersede the handful of *S-30* boats. The new badge shows the heavier and more common *S-38* Class. The wreath of this badge has a flatter base and the oak leaves are of a smaller and more delicate design. The tie has a more pronounced central spine and the two outer lines are wider and join the central spine with a very fine line. The eagle surmounting the wreath is much larger and, in comparison with the stumpy-winged version of the First Type badge, it has a longer wingspan. The swastika in this badge is found in two distinct styles – it can either be solid or cut out between the arms – and it is placed beneath the inner edge line of the wreath.

The other main distinguishing factor is

that in this type the S-boat is cutting through three distinct low waves. This time the boat breaks the wreath so that the prow forms part of the outer edge design, while the wake breaks the outer edge of the wreath on the opposite side. The badge measures 60mm from the base to the top of the eagle's head and 53mm across the badge from the tip of the prow to the edge of the wake. The wreath measures 8mm and the eagle's wingspan is 36.5mm, with the height of the eagle and swastika being 20mm.

The reverse has the maker's logo or address on it with a horizontal or vertical pin. Again in the case of the horizontal pin the little hook is found at the top, which safeguarded the attachment to the tunic as previously described.

It was presented in a blue box with blue flock base and white silk lid liner, through to the paper packet in varying colours, with the derivation of the badge printed in black on the front.

This is another badge designed by Wilhelm Ernst Peekhaus of Berlin but this time it was in conjunction with Korvettenkapitän Rudolf Peterson and the resultant design was introduced into service in January 1943. It was worn on the left breast pocket, underneath the Iron Cross First Class or like award.

The criteria for the award were exactly the same as for the First Type badge.

Schnellboot War Badge – French Type

Instituted: 30 May 1941
Rarity: rare
Known maker(s)/markings: unmarked –
Mourgeon (Paris), Bacqueville

This badge is of the French-constructed type with the distinctive wreath, eagle and swastika. The badge is of the same general design as the S-boat Badge First Type. It measures 55mm from the base to the top of the eagle's head and 41mm across. The width of the wreath is 7mm, the eagle's wingspan is 27mm and the height of the eagle and swastika are 14mm.

The reverse is hollow-struck and has the distinctive French pin, hinge and hook con-

struction. The whole of the reverse is silvered. The container in which the badge was awarded was a buff box in two parts with the edges stapled together and the badge was wrapped in white tissue paper.

The criteria for this award were identical to those of the previous two badges.

Schnellboot War Badge with Diamonds – First Type

Number awarded: 1 (?)
Rarity: extremely rare
Known maker(s)/markings: Schwerin

This badge was not a national award but was a personal presentation or award from the commander of the German Navy to particularly successful commanders of the S-boats who patrolled the English Channel. The badge was designed by Peekhaus and was produced by the firm of Schwerin of Berlin. It took the form of the First Type S-boat Badge, but it was in this case constructed from solid silver of .800 grade and finely gilded. The swastika was slightly larger than that found in the standard badge. In this were set nine rose-cut diamonds, which were set directly into the arms of the swastika. It was awarded at an informal ceremony after the recipient had received his Knight's Cross with Oak Leaves and was not accom-

panied by a citation. One of the recipients of the S-boat War Badge with Diamonds, Korvettenkapitän Friedrich Kemnade, stated that the award was the prerogative of the Admiral Inspekteur der Marine rather than Hitler. He further had this to say,

'All wearers of the Oak Leaves to the Ritterkreuz and [higher grade decorations] above the Oak Leaves were invited by Grossadmiral Raeder for lunch in his home on which occasion he passed the Schnellboot and U-bootskriegsabzeichen to the newly decorated wearers. There was no award document since these officers were in possession of the award document passed out by the OKM. The gems in the swastika were not real diamonds, but splinters of diamonds.'

It is probable that Kapitänleutnant Werne Toniges who received the Oak Leaves on 13 November 1942 was the only recipient of the First Type.

Photo 188: Schnellboot War Badge with Diamonds – First Type.

Photo 189: Schnellboot War Badge with Diamonds – Second Type.

Photo 190: Reverse of the Schnellboot War Badge with Diamonds – Second Type.

Photo 191: Schnellboot War Badge with Diamonds – Variation. This piece is controversial and is not normal manufacturing practice.

Kapitänleutnant Werne Toniges	13 November 1942
Oberleutnant-zur-See Siegfried Wuppermann	14 April 1943
Korvettenkapitän Friedrich Kemnade	23 May 1943
Korvettenkapitän George Christiansen	13 November 1943
Korvettenkapitän Klaus Feldt	1 January 1944
Korvettenkapitän Bernd Klug	1 January 1944
Kapitän-zur-See Rudolf Peterson	13 June 1944
Kapitänleutnant Göpz Freiherr von Mirbach	14 June 1944

author but in correspondence Admiral Dönitz stated that the badge simply came in a protective jeweller's box.

Those who were awarded the badge are listed above.

Schnellboot War Badge with Diamonds – Variation

Rarity: unique
Known maker(s)/markings: M.003

There is a unique example of this badge with the difference that the space above the boat is solid, and the field that this creates is pebbled. This badge was produced in bronze and finely gilded. The swastika and diamonds are formed as in the former badge. The reverse of the

Schnellboot War Badge with Diamonds – Second Type

Number awarded: 7 (?)
Rarity: extremely rare
Known maker(s)/markings: Schwerin

This had the same design as the Second Type S-boat Badge, but was made from solid silver of .800 grade and finely gilded. The swastika was slightly larger than that found in the standard badge. In this were set nine rose-cut diamonds, which were set directly into the arms of the swastika.

These badges, as far as research can ascertain, were awarded only eight times, and were additional honours for holders of the Knight's Cross with Oak Leaves. The type of container used for these badges is unknown to the

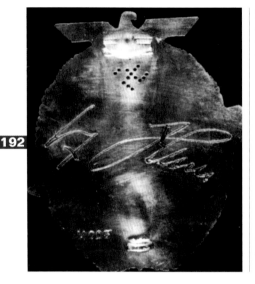

192

badge is numbered 'M.003' and has Hitler's signature on it. The status of this badge is unknown. One theory is that this could be a wear copy for general use.

High Seas Fleet War Badge

Instituted: 30 April 1941
Rarity: scarce
Known maker(s)/markings: unmarked, Adolf Bock, Schwerin, Ausf. Schwerin Berlin in conjunction with Adolf Bock designer's mark, Fredrich Orth, FO, R.S. & S., R.S. (both angular and round forms of the letters), L/21

This badge has as its central design a head-on view of a capital ship at full steam, ploughing through a sea and producing a bow wave. This

193

Photo 192: Reverse of the Schnellboot War Badge with Diamonds – Variation. It shows Adolf Hitler's signature. This was not a national award but a personal presentation from the Commander of the German Navy.

Photo 193: High Seas Fleet War Badge.

Photo 194: Reverse of the High Seas Fleet War Badge.

Photo 195: High Seas Fleet War Badge struck in zinc.

Photo 196: Reverse of the High Seas Fleet War Badge. This shows the vertical pin and maker's mark, RS – Rudolf Souval.

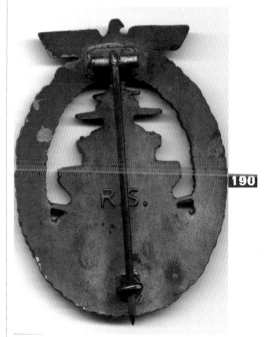

is passing through an oak-leaf wreath, with a large-winged eagle at the top of the wreath. The base of the wreath has a ribbon tie in the form of an X with an acorn in the upper and lower V formed by the tie and, on either side, eight bunches of two oak leaves. The tip of each leaf has a single acorn positioned to the outer or inner edge of the wreath. The height of the badge from the base to the top of the eagle's head is 57mm and the width is 44mm, while the width of the wreath is 7mm. The eagle's wingspan is 31mm. The wreath is gilded and the ship and sea are dark oxidised silver, with some of the highlights being polished. The gilt on the wreath has tended to be absorbed over time, giving the appearance of a silver wreath, but this should not be confused with a variant badge, which may have a gold or a silver wreath.

The reverse of the badge is flat with a dished effect behind the battleship. There are a number of types of hinges and pins, but the hooks are nearly always of the C-form. The reverse is blackened along with the hinge, pin and hook assemblies. The badges by Bock and Schwerin are of particularly high quality with heavy pins and quality hinge and hook construction, while those of Friedrich Orth tend to be of inferior quality, with a thin needle pin.

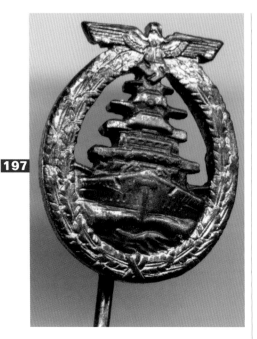

197

198

Photo 197: High Seas Fleet War Badge – Miniature Stick Pin.

Photo 198: High Seas Fleet War Badge in cloth. The construction is interesting in the fact the wreath and eagle are executed in yellow while the ship is in silver bullion.

In the case of this maker the hook was cast with the badge and, as the badge gets older, this tends to crystallise. In this brittle state it is very prone to being broken off.

A cloth version was authorised for wear on the blue uniform. It has a yellow cotton wreath and eagle, with the battleship and sea worked in grey cotton with the highlights in lighter grey or off-white cotton thread.

This badge was introduced on 30 April 1941 at the direction of Grossadmiral Raeder to recognise the sea actions by larger vessels of the Kriegsmarine. The designer of the badge and principal maker was Adolf Bock of Berlin. It was worn on the left breast pocket, underneath the Iron Cross First Class or like award.

The container in which better quality badges were awarded was a blue box with blue flock base and white silk lid lining, with the name of the badge stencilled in silver on the lid top. Inferior quality badges were presented in a grey paper packet with the name of the badge printed on the front.

The criteria for the award were one or more of:

1.   Twelve weeks' service on a battleship or cruiser;

2.   The qualifying period of service could be reduced if the recipient had been wounded;

3.   The qualifying period of service could be reduced if the cruise had been successful;

4.   Service in a major vessel for which no other award badge could be given.

The award of the High Seas Fleet War Badge began with a recommendation from the ship's captain and had to be approved by a Kommodore or Konteradmiral.

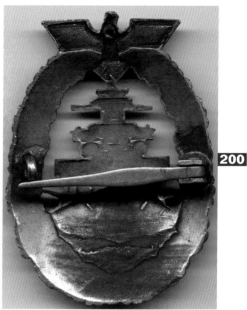

High Seas Fleet War Badge – French Type

Rarity: scarce
Known maker(s)/markings: unmarked – Mourgeon (Paris), Bacqueville

This badge is identical in most respects to the former badge. The differences are in the way that the wreath is produced. In this case the oak leaves are of a more offset pattern giving a rougher appearance to both the inner and outer edges of the wreath. The eagle has a rounder form of fletching to the underside of the wing and the wingspan of the eagle is reduced. The badge measures 55mm from the base to the top of the eagle's head, the width is 41mm and that of the wreath 8mm. The eagle's wingspan is 27mm.

The reverse is semi-stamped and there is a horizontal hinge, pin and hook of the French style, which has been previously described, with a hook mounted behind the eagle. The reverse is finished in silver. These badges are scarce and desirable.

The container is similar to the original version. It is a buff box with the corners stapled together.

High Seas Fleet War Badge with Diamonds

Rarity: extremely rare
Known maker(s)/markings: unmarked

An example of the High Seas Fleet War Badge First Type was produced in .800 grade solid silver. The swastika in this badge is slightly enlarged and 14 rose-cut diamonds are set directly into it. Why this badge was produced is uncertain but it is likely that it was made as an additional reward for men who won the Oak Leaves during service, which would have also qualified them for the High Seas Fleet War Badge. This would have then logically come in line with the other diamond-set medals for the Navy. However, there were no examples of the Oak Leaves being awarded for big-ship service, so the award never became necessary. Thus the badge is still surrounded in uncertainty.

Photo 199: High Seas Fleet War Badge – French Type.

Photo 200: Reverse of the High Seas Fleet War Badge – French Type. This shows the typical pin hinge and hook of the Bacqueville-made badges.

Instituted: 24 April 1941
Rarity: scarce
Known maker(s)/markings: 'Schwerin Berlin' in relief (without '68'), FO, R.S. (both angular and round forms of the letters), L/21

Wilhelm Ernst Peekhaus of Berlin produced this badge on request from Grossadmiral Raeder to reward service on auxiliary cruisers (*Hilfskreuzer*). It was introduced on 24 April 1941. In its early forms the badge was constructed in two parts, and the base was of solid brass. This was then burnished to give

201

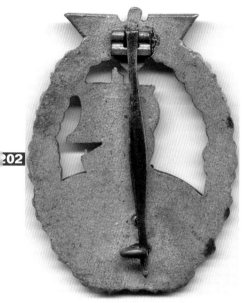

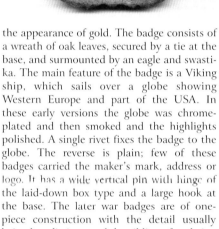
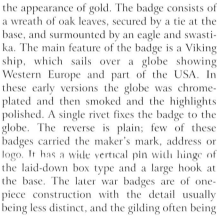

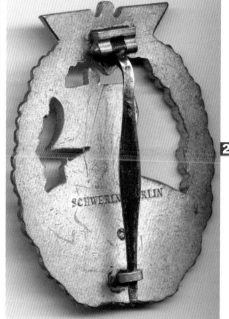

the appearance of gold. The badge consists of a wreath of oak leaves, secured by a tie at the base, and surmounted by an eagle and swastika. The main feature of the badge is a Viking ship, which sails over a globe showing Western Europe and part of the USA. In these early versions the globe was chromeplated and then smoked and the highlights polished. A single rivet fixes the badge to the globe. The reverse is plain; few of these badges carried the maker's mark, address or logo. It has a wide vertical pin with hinge of the laid-down box type and a large hook at the base. The later war badges are of one-piece construction with the detail usually being less distinct, and the gilding often being

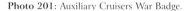

Photo 201: Auxiliary Cruisers War Badge.

Photo 202: Reverse of the Auxiliary Cruisers War Badge. This is an unmarked version.

Photo 203: Auxiliary Cruisers War Badge by Schwerin, Berlin.

Photo 204: Reverse of the Auxiliary Cruisers War Badge showing the marker's mark: Schwerin, Berlin.

absorbed, giving a rather dull and lifeless appearance. These badges are usually with a vertical pin and the maker's mark, which is often that of Fredrick Orth.

The criteria for the award were one or more of:

1. Participation in a successful long-distance voyage;

2. Outstanding leadership;

3. Being wounded in the course of duty on a long-distance voyage.

The German Naval attaché in Tokyo, Admiral Paul Wenneker, commissioned two Japanese firms to undertake the manufacture of awards, to fulfil the need for when there was no on-hand stock readily available. This gave rise to the badge shown here.

The badge was rendered with a citation, which normally came with a facsimile of the badge at its head, name of the badge in the middle and commander's signature and stamp at the bottom. At first the badges came in a blue box with a dark blue base and white silk lid lining; the later awards were rendered in blue paper packets with the name of the badge printed in black on the front.

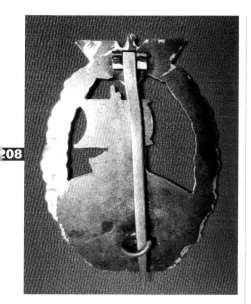

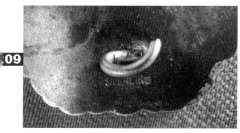

Auxiliary Cruisers and their Fates

Atlantis	sunk by HMS *Devonshire*
Michel	sunk by USS *Tarpon*
Stier	sunk by SS *Stephen Hopkins*
Komet	sunk by British destroyers off Cherbourg
Orion	returned safely to Germany
Thor	destroyed by fire at the port of Yokohama
Kormoran	sunk by HMAS *Sydney*
Pinguin	sunk by HMS *Cornwall*
Widder	returned safely to Germany

Auxiliary Cruiser War Badge – French Type

Rarity: scarce
Known maker(s)/markings: unmarked – Mourgeon (Paris), Bacqueville

The Viking ship on this badge has numerous small differences from the former badge, which distinguish it clearly, as does the design of the globe. This badge was manufactured in

Photo 205: Auxiliary Cruisers War Badge miniature stick pin.

Photo 206: Reverse of the Auxiliary Cruisers War Badge stick pin.

Photo 207: Auxiliary Cruisers War Badge made in Japan.

Photo 208: Reverse of the Auxiliary Cruisers War Badge made in Japan.

Photo 209: Close-up of the silver mark used Sterling.

Photo 210: Auxiliary Cruisers War Badge – French Type.

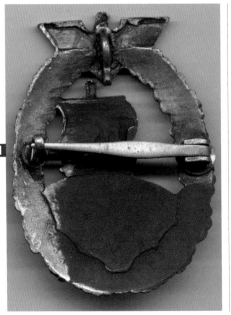

one piece, the wreath again being in the distinctive French design with the variant eagle. The reverse is hollow-struck with the French style of pin. The badge came boxed in a buff, two-part box with the edges stapled together and the badge wrapped in white tissue paper.

Auxiliary Cruiser War Badge with Diamonds

Number awarded: 2
Rarity: extremely rare
Known maker(s)/markings: unmarked

This badge was identical to the Auxiliary Cruiser Badge in construction but was produced in solid silver of .800 grade. The wreath and eagle are finely gilded, the ship and globe being polished. This badge was introduced by Grossadmiral Raeder in January 1942 and was to be used like the other diamond awards as a further mark of favour when the recipient had

Photo 211: Reverse of the Auxiliary Cruisers War Badge – French Type. This shows the typical pin hinge and hook of the Bacqueville-made badges.

Photo 212: Auxiliary Cruisers War Badge with Diamonds.

Photo 213: Blockade Runner Badge.

received the Oak Leaves to his Knight's Cross.

This badge was awarded to Kapitän-zur-See Bernhard Rogge, commander of the *Atlantis*, which had been a particularly successful raider. A second example was awarded to Kapitän-zur-See Ernst Felix Kruder of the *Pinguin*. It is also thought that the badge was to have been awarded to Kapitän-zur-See Hellmuth Ruckteschell of the *Michel*, but it has been reported that he never actually received the award.

The badge did not come with an award citation and the type of box in which it was presented is unknown. The only interesting variation is that Rogge had the pin of his badge removed and a screw post put on the reverse to make it more secure while he was wearing it on his tunic.

Blockade Runner Badge

Instituted: 1 April 1941
Rarity: common
Known maker(s)/markings: R.S. (both angular and round forms of the letters), 'Ausf. Schwerin Berlin' in conjunction with Placzek designer's mark

Hitler instituted this badge to recognise the courage of Merchant Navy personnel who were breaking the British blockade. The badge was designed by Otto Placzek of Berlin and introduced on 1 April 1941. The first recipient was Hugo Olendorff on 1 July 1941. At the same time Olendorff received an award document.

The badge shows a liner breaking a chain, to symbolise the blockade. The badge has an

Photo 214: Reverse of the Blockade Runner Badge showing the vertical pin.

Photo 215: Reverse of the Blockade Runner Badge showing the vertical round needle pin.

Photo 216: Blockade Runner Badge with Civilian Wear badge in presentation case.

Photo 217: Blockade Runner Badge with miniature stick pin in case.

Photo 218: Citation for the Blockade Runner Badge. This was awarded to Masch. Wärter Kurt Gebbert on 8 June 1944. Der Oberbefehlshaber der Kriegsmarine, Dönitz Großadmiral.

The criteria for the award were:

1. Bringing a ship into a German or German-held port, after successfully running the Allied blockade;

2. Having scuttled a ship to avoid capture;

3. Having served aboard a ship lost through enemy action while at sea;

4. For displaying daring or courage in preventing a ship from falling into enemy hands.

The badge was awarded with a citation, which usually had a facsimile of the badge on it. This can either be found at the top of the paper or in some cases at the bottom. The relevant awarding authority was at the bottom with its stamp and signature. The badge was awarded with a miniature version for wear on civilian clothes, in a blue box with blue lid liner and with a base that could either be of blue velvet or flocking.

Im Namen des
Führers und Obersten Befehlshabers
der Wehrmacht
verleihe ich
dem

Masch.Wärter

Kurt Gebbert

das

Abzeichen für Blockadebrecher

Den 8.Juni 1944

Der Oberbefehlshaber der Kriegsmarine

Dönitz
Großadmiral

Für die Richtigkeit

(Dienstgrad und Dienststellung)

overall grey appearance but the chain is high-lighted in white, as is the eagle, which forms the prow motif of the ship. In some cases this motif is silver with the highlights polished. The reverse usually has the maker's mark or name and address and a broad vertical pin. It is also encountered with a thin needle pin, which can be either vertical or horizontal. In the cases of the horizontal pin construction, a small hook is found at the top of the badge.

Recommendations for the award in the case of the Merchant Navy came from the Reich Commission for Sea Travel. In the case of the Kriegsmarine, senior officers recommended a man who had fulfilled the necessary criteria for approval by the Commander-in-Chief.

Photo 219: Blockade Runner Badge – Civilian Wear.

Photo 220: Reverse of the Blockade Runner Badge – Civilian Wear.

Photo 221: Blockade Runner Badge – Miniature stick pin.

Photo 222: Reverse of the Blockade Runner Badge – Miniature stick pin.

Photo 223: Coastal Artillery War Badge.

Blockade Runner Badge – Civilian Wear

Instituted: 1 April 1941
Rarity: common
Known maker(s)/markings: unmarked, 'Ausf. Schwerin Berlin' in conjunction with Placzek designer's mark

This badge was identical in every respect to the former; save that it was approximately one-quarter of the size of the large one. There are, in fact, a considerable number of varieties of size to this miniature. However, these should not be considered as representing official awarded types of civilian stickpin, but rather those, which one could buy as any other form of miniature for general wear on civilian clothing. The reverse has a vertical stickpin and sometimes a maker's mark. This badge was to be worn on civilian or non-military clothing, either on a ship or off duty ashore.

Coastal Artillery War Badge

Instituted: 24 June 1941
Rarity: common
Known maker(s)/markings:
'Schwerin Berlin' in relief
(without '68'), W (within a
circle), FFL, FFL (with date),
R.S. (both angular and round
forms of the letters)

Grossadmiral Raeder decided
that land-based naval personnel
should have a badge to recognise their importance in anti-
aircraft and coastal defence.
The designer was the firm of
Otto Placzek of Berlin and the
badge was introduced on 24
June 1941.

The badge shows a land-
based naval gun with the sea as
the background. An eagle with
downswept wings surmounts
the wreath of oak leaves round
the gun and is similar to those
found on Army badges. This
may have been to show that

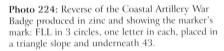

22

Photo 224: Reverse of the Coastal Artillery War Badge produced in zinc and showing the marker's mark: FLL in 3 circles, one letter in each, placed in a triangle slope and underneath 43.

Photo 225: Coastal Artillery Badge produced in Tomback.

Photo 226: Reverse of the Coastal Artillery Badge showing the maker Schwerin, Berlin.

Photo 227: Coastal Artillery War Badge miniature stick pin.

Photo 228: Reverse of the Coastal Artillery War Badge miniature stick pin.

recipients were, in fact, land-based as opposed to their seafaring colleagues. However, that observation is just a supposition.

The reverse is flat with a wide vertical pin and usually the maker's mark is also found. The wreath is finely gilded and the gun is of a smoked dark grey. Badges were made in high quality nickel during the early period of the war but, as the war progressed, the usual debasement occurred with pot or monkey metal being used. Some badges are of very high quality and have no gilding on them whatsoever, which has given rise to some collectors believing that there was in fact a silver grade. However, this is incorrect.

The criteria for the award were one or more of:

1.   A display of leadership relevant to the position that the recipient held in the gun crew;

2.   A single act of 'meritorious service' for which no other award could be rendered;

3.   If the recipient had been killed in action, contracted illness or was killed by accident in the line of duty;

128

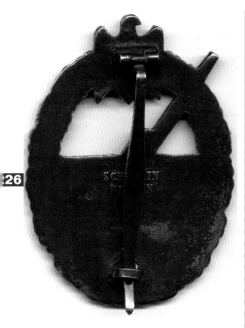

226

227

4. Service as a member of a gun crew when the crew had amassed eight points.

The points were calculated as:

a. Two points for shooting down an aircraft unassisted;

b. One point if assisted by another gun crew;

c. For non-gun crewmembers – searchlight, fire control, sound-locator and radio-operator personnel – eligibility also required eight points. These were accumulated at the rate of half point for each first detection of an incoming aircraft or flight.

228

The badge was awarded with a citation, which usually had a facsimile of the badge at its top, the name of the badge in the middle and the company commander's signature and stamp at the bottom. The badge was usually presented in a paper packet (which varied in colour) with the name of the badge printed on the front.

229

Coastal Artillery War Badge – French Type

Instituted: 24 June 1941
Rarity: scarce
Known maker(s)/markings: unmarked – Mourgeon (Paris), Bacqueville

This badge was produced in France and takes the general form of the previous badge. The main difference is in the oak leaves of the wreath, which have a rougher appearance to both the inner and outer edges of the wreath. The gun is of a slightly different design and the eagle surmounting the wreath is a smaller version than on the original type. The obverse is semi-struck with the negative of the reverse and it has a broad horizontal pin of the French style already described, and a hook behind the eagle's body. This badge is quite rare and considered to be desirable in collecting circles.

The badge came in a buff-coloured box with detachable lid, with the corners stapled together.

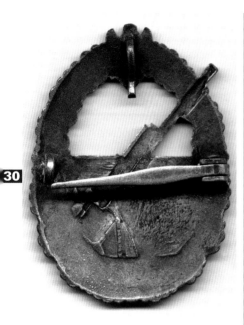

Instituted: 19 November 1944
Rarity: very rare
Known maker(s)/markings:
unmarked, 11

Grossadmiral Dönitz introduced this badge in November 1944 to recognise further acts of valour for the holders of War Badges who would not have the chance of winning an equivalent front clasp. That is to say, he decided that a general clasp would be introduced, rather than a special clasp for each type of badge, as was the case for the Luftwaffe, and it was to fit into the same scheme as that of the Army.

In the original design the badge has an oval centrepiece with a chain forming a wreath or outer edge of a central motif of an anchor. The chain is attached at the top of an anchor. The base has crossed swords and the centre is an anchor surmounted by a naval eagle with a swastika in its talons. The oval chain wreath has a horizontal oak-leaf cluster on either side. This beautifully designed badge was never placed into production, although a few 'proof' examples were struck. The badge that was put into production differed quite considerably and took the form of an anchor in a plain circle, with a similar but not so striking oak-leaf cluster emanating from either side. Crude examples of the latter badge were produced in the field. However, some finely produced examples have recently come to light and been offered on the market.

Photo 229: Coastal Artillery War Badge – French Type.

Photo 230: Reverse of the Coastal Artillery War Badge – French Type. This shows the typical pin hinge and hook of the Bacqueville-made badges.

Photo 231: Naval Combat Clasp – first proposed design.

232

Photo 232: This is a photo of a *Prinz Eugen* crewman. The national insignia over the right breast has been removed as is the national insignia on the cap. He has the marine front Naval Combat Clasp Marine – Frontspange on the tunic and the cap tally. Since the tally was issued on 5 January 1946, the photo had to be taken after that date. The ship still had a partial German crew aboard when she arrived in San Diego, California, on 1 May 1946 at which point the German crew were disbanded. The exact date of the photo is not known but, it would appear to be taken by a German photographer (as indicated on the bottom right of the image), it was most probably taken either prior to mid-January 1946 while the ship was still moored in Wilhelmshaven, Germany, before sailing to the US or when the sailor returned to Germany in 1946.

Photo 233: Naval Combat Clasp. This example was bought by David Littlejohn from Dr Klietmann in 1950.

Photo 234: Reverse of the Naval Combat Clasp.

Photo 235: Naval Combat Clasp handmade during the war.

Photo 236: Reverse of the handmade Naval Combat Clasp.

The criteria for the award were:

1. It was necessary to perform five times whatever was requisite to be awarded the relevant Naval Award Badge;

2. For special service or valour for which a War Badge would have been awarded.

The badge was rendered with a citation but was presented in an ignominious cellophane wrapper.

237

Photo 237: Small Battle Unit Combat Badge – Fourth Class.

Photo 238: Small Battle Unit Combat Badge – Third Class.

Photo 239: Small Battle Unit Combat Badge – Third Class. This badge was in the collection bought back by Lieutenant Commander Albert McRae.

Photo 240: Small Battle Unit Combat Badge – Second Class.

Photo 241: Small Battle Unit Combat Badge – First Class.

Small Battle Unit Combat Badge – Fourth Class

Instituted: 13 November 1944
Rarity: rare
Known maker(s)/markings: unmarked

This series of badges was designed by Ottfried Neubeker and was instituted on 13 November 1944. The Fourth Class badge was to reward service and leadership of the small battle units or frogmen groups. The badge had a blue cloth background and featured a swordfish in a rope circle executed in yellow stitching. This grade was given to men who had planned an action that had ended successfully.

There is a plausible theory that the badge (in all its various grades) was made in yellow cotton for NCOs and gold bullion for officers.

It is not known if any of the Small Battle Unit Badges (in any grade) were awarded with a citation, or just a note in the pay book of the recipient.

Small Battle Unit Combat Badge – Third Class

Instituted: 13 November 1944
Rarity: rare
Known maker(s)/markings: unmarked

23

The Third Class badge is identical in design, but in this case a sword is added at 45 degrees, which passes through the badge, with the handle to the base of the badge.

This badge was awarded for bravery in action either on land or sea, as a member of a group or as an individual when part of a raiding party.

Small Battle Unit Combat Badge – Second Class

Instituted: 13 November 1944
Rarity: rare
Known maker(s)/markings: unmarked

The Second Class again has the same design but with two swords at 45 degree angles (and thus crossing at 90 degrees) with the hilts both to the bottom of the badge. The criteria for the award were also the same, but this badge was to reward the recipient at a higher level.

Small Battle Unit Combat Badge – First Class

Instituted: 13 November 1944
Rarity: rare
Known maker(s)/markings: unmarked

The First Class is identical in its general design and the criteria for the award are the same as those of the junior classes, but this badge was to reward further acts of service or valour. The badge was again a swordfish in a rope circle but to the two crossed swords previously described was added a third sword, which passed through the badge vertically.

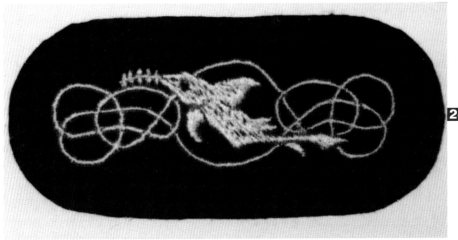

246

Small Battle Unit Combat Badge, Bar – Bronze, Silver, Gold Class

Rarity: extremely rare
Known maker(s)/markings: unmarked

These clasps were introduced as additional rewards for the units that were engaged in one-man submarine and frogmen operations. The badges were metal with, as a central motif, a swordfish swimming to the left (the opposite of the cloth badges) within an oval wreath made of rope which runs round to produce the two sides of the oval. On either side of the oval the rope forms the elongated part of the clasp. The rope is segmented between each part so that it gives a delicate, interlaced appearance. The reverse has a long broad fluted pin that runs horizontally along the badge.

The criteria for the award were:

1. Four actions entitled the recipient to the Bronze Class;

2. Seven actions entitled the recipient to the Silver Class;

3. Ten actions entitled the recipient to the Gold Class.

There is some doubt if this badge, in any of

Photo 242: Small Battle Unit Combat Badge – bar, bronze.

Photo 243: Reverse of the Small Battle Unit Combat Badge – bar, bronze.

Photo 244: Small Battle Unit Combat Badge – bar, silver.

Photo 245: Reverse of the Small Battle Unit Combat Badge – bar, silver.

Photo 246: Small Battle Unit Combat Badge in cloth.

its grades, were awarded. The majority of badges that turn up in collecting circles are in fact the 1957 badge, which was permitted to be worn by the Federal West German government. As the design is identical in both these series, it is difficult to determine which was produced before the end of hostilities in 1945.

If a citation accompanied this range of badges it is unknown, as is the form of protective packet or box in which the badge would have been awarded.

Naval Long Service Medal, 4 Years' Service

Instituted: 16 March 1936
Rarity: common
Known maker(s)/markings: L/13, L/15

This award is a round medal 30mm across. It has a raised edge line and on the flat field produced is placed the inscription, in raised Gothic capitals that run from 7 o'clock to 4 o'clock, 'TREUE DIENSTE IN DER WEHRMACHT' – 'Loyal Service in the Armed Forces'. The Wehrmacht eagle is placed on the field at the centre. The eagle's wings are partially opened, with its head looking to the viewer's right and a swastika clutched in its claws. At the top of the medal is placed an eyelet, through which runs the ribbon ring. The medal is 2.5mm thick and the overall colour is matt patinated silver. The medal is produced in varying types of base metal.

The reverse has a similar raised edge line and on the flat field produced, inset by 1mm, is a circle of oak leaves in the form of a wreath. The circle has a solid inner and outer edge line with a tie, at 12 and 6 o'clock respectively. Lines, giving the effect of ribbons wound round the wreath, form the ties. There are a number of variations in the designs of these ties and I have five slight variants in my collection. From the lower one, on either side, run five oak leaves with raised veins. On to the flat field at the centre is placed a large raised Arabic number 4. Professor Richard Klein of Munich designed the medal.

The ribbon is cornflower blue and can measure 27–35mm in width. The finish can vary from a plain matt to a bright watered effect. To denote the service to which the recipient was attached, a silver eagle was added to the ribbon. In the case of the Army and Navy, this was the straight, outstretched-winged national emblem. It measures 25mm across by 10.5mm high. However, the eagles employed on the ribbon bar were sometimes used incorrectly on the medal ribbon. These measure 15mm by 9mm and 15mm by 8mm, while the Luftwaffe employed a flying eagle that measures 18mm by 13mm. Again, smaller ones are encountered measuring 14mm by 10mm and 11mm by 8mm. It must be stressed that there is a wide variation in the sizes of these emblems and readers may have variations not listed. This is not to be considered unusual.

The medal was worn either on a furled court-mounted ribbon or on a medal ribbon bar. It was authorised to be worn on parade or walking-out-dress uniform. At other times a ribbon bar was worn above the left breast pocket and on it was worn the relevant emblem denoting branch of service, as well as the grade of the award.

The medal was awarded for the completion of four years' service and during the early

Photo 247: Naval Long Service Medal – 4 Years' Service.

Photo 248: Reverse of the Naval Long Service Medal – 4 Years' Service.

Photo 249: Naval Long Service Medal – 12 Years' Service.

Photo 250: Reverse of the Naval Long Service Medal – 12 Years' Service.

years of its institution was bestowed in a special ceremony by the commanding officer. With the outbreak of war, actual issue of the service award ceased. The 4 Year Medal could be worn on its own or in conjunction with the 12 Year Medal or the 18 Year Cross. It was decreed that only two long service awards could be worn at the same time.

The medal was rendered in a green paper packet with the title of the medal upon it, 'Dienst_aus_zeichnung mit Hoheits_abze-ichen u. Band IV'. The packet was, in some cases, just a clear cellophane protective wrapper.

Naval Long Service Medal, 12 Years' Service

Instituted: 16 March 1936
Rarity: common
Known maker(s)/markings: L/13, L/15

The design of this medal is identical to the 4 Year Medal on the obverse while the reverse is equally the same, save that the 4 is replaced by an Arabic number 12. The ribbon is also the same, with the same form of eagle applied to denote branch of service. However, the whole of the medal including the eagle is finished in gold.

There is, however, an interesting obverse variation that has no outer edge line and slightly larger gothic lettering. The eagle is also slightly different in that it has a more pronounced head. The reverse is identical to the standard form and the medal is 3mm thick and made of a heavier high-grade metal alloy.

The medal was awarded for the completion of 12 years' service. The 12 Year Medal was

worn in conjunction with the 4 Year Medal, and in conjunction with the 25 Year Cross and the 40 Year Cross.

The medal was rendered in a green paper packet with the title of the medal printed upon it, 'Dienstauszeichnung mit Hoheitsabzeichen u. Band III'. The packet was sometimes just a clear cellophane protective wrapper.

139

251

Photo 252: Reverse of the Naval Long Service Medal – 18 Years' Service.

The reverse of the cross is identical to the obverse, save that an Arabic number 18 replaces the eagle. Professor Richard Klein of Munich designed the cross, like the medals. The overall colour of the cross and the relevant ribbon eagle is silver. From the upper arm of the cross is an eyelet through which is placed the ribbon suspension ring. The ribbon is identical to that described in the 4 Year Medal.

The cross was awarded for the completion of 18 years' service. The 18 Year Cross was worn with the 4 Year Medal.

The cross was rendered in a green carton, which was compartmentalised and finished inside with a mouse-grey flocking, with an Arabic 18 surrounded by an oak-leaf wreath stencilled on to the lid in silver.

Naval Long Service Cross, 18 Years' Service

Instituted: 16 March 1936
Rarity: scarce
Known maker(s)/markings: L/13, L/15

This award is in the form of a Finnish or Greek (St George's) Cross with slightly widening arms. It measures 36mm across and has a 15mm central medallion. Round the arms of the cross is a raised edge line. Indented by 0.5mm is a further one, and a similar line indented again by 0.5mm follows this. The central field of the arms of the cross is raised, gently bevelled and slopes down towards the outer edge line of the arms of the cross. The central medallion has a similar raised outer edge line and a similar one indented by 0.5mm. The central field is finely pebbled and is slightly convexed. On this is superimposed a raised Wehrmacht eagle.

252

Naval Long Service Cross, 25 Years' Service

Instituted: 16 March 1936
Rarity: scarce
Known maker(s)/markings: L/13, L/15

This award, like its predecessor, is a St George's Cross. It measures 40mm across and also has an 18mm central medallion. Round the arms of the cross runs a 1.5mm raised border. The field of the arms of the cross has a fine raised pebbling. The central medallion has a fine, raised edge line and a similar one indented by 0.5mm. The field of the tramline produced is plain, while the central field has a similar fine, raised pebbled finish. On to this is superimposed the Wehrmacht eagle. From the upper arm is an eyelet, through which passes the ribbon ring.

The reverse of the cross is identical to the obverse, save that an Arabic number 25 replaces the Wehrmacht eagle. Professor Richard Klein of Munich designed the cross. The overall colour of the cross and the relevant ribbon eagle is gold. The ribbon is identical to that described for the 4 Year Medal.

The 25 Year Cross was worn in conjunction with the 8 Year Medal.

The cross was rendered in a green box with a press-stud catch. The outer green covering is simulated leather, while the inside lid liner is white silk and the base is compartmentalised and finished in mouse-grey velvet. On the lid is stencilled the Arabic number 25 in an oak-leaf wreath, finished in gold.

Photo 253: Naval Long Service Medal – 25 Years' Service.

Photo 254: Reverse of the Naval Long Service Medal – 25 Years' Service.

Photo 255: Ribbon Bar belonging to GrandAdmiral Karl Dönitz showing the long service medals with ribbon emblems.

Naval Long Service Cross, 40 Years' Service

Instituted: 10 March 1939
Rarity: rare
Known maker(s)/markings: unmarked

This award was an oak-leaf spray, which was added to the ribbon of the 25 Year Cross. The spray measures 34mm across the tips and is 17mm high. The base has a ribbon curling downwards from a knot at the centre. Extending from the knot, in a V-form, are two oak leaves. From each side is a larger leaf overlapping two smaller ones. The area between the ribbons and the leaves is usually solid, but in some cases can be found voided. In collecting terms this latter version is regarded as less desirable than the former. The emblem is attached to the ribbon by two flat pins through the ribbon. The reverse of the emblem is plain and flat. The overall colour of the emblem is matt gold.

The emblem was awarded for the completion of 40 years' service. The 40 Year Cross was worn with the 8 Year Medal.

The emblem was presented in a small green box. It is possible to encounter the cross with the emblem attached and in a red hard case with a gilt Arabic 40 within a wreath of oak leaves. This case had a press-stud catch and the inner lid liner was of white silk, while the lower portion was segmented and finished in a maroon velvet liner. This is similar to that employed for the Faithful Service Decoration for 40 Years' Service.

Badge for Long Service as a Civilian Employee of the Army or Navy

Instituted: 30 April 1936
Rarity: scarce
Known maker(s)/markings: unmarked

This badge takes the form of an eagle with outstretched wings, which measures 30mm across. In its talons it holds a round oak-leaf wreath with a tie at the base. The oak leaves are formed in bunches of two, seven in each side of the wreath. The field produced is finely pebbled and on this is superimposed a raised swastika. The whole design is placed on a round wreath of oak leaves, which are irregularly aligned. The top of the wreath is semi-closed. This measures 28mm high. The whole of the badge is finely struck from fine zinc or copper that is gilded. The reverse is plain with a vertical stickpin.

The badge was introduced to 'promote the feeling of belonging to the armed forces' by an order dated 30 April 1936. This permitted the wearing of a distinctive badge on the left lapel of the civilian jacket or coat by all civilian employees of both the Army and Navy. Personnel working for the Luftwaffe, still a clandestine organisation banned by the Treaty of Versailles, were excluded at this time. The employees could be both 'salaried and paid hourly', giving rise to an informal title with this meaning used for the award, 'Angestellte und Arbeite'. The badge is as described above but in this case it is in a silver colour. It was originally planned that the badge be stamped from German silver; however, because of production difficulties, it was produced in silver-plated copper or similar metal. This was

Photo 256: Naval Long Service Medal – 40 Years' Service.

Photo 257: Reverse of the Naval Long Service Medal – 40 Years' Service. The 25-year medal was worn with the addition of an oakleaf spray to the ribbon, (see 256).

Photo 258: Badge for Long Service as a Civilian Employee of the Army or Navy.

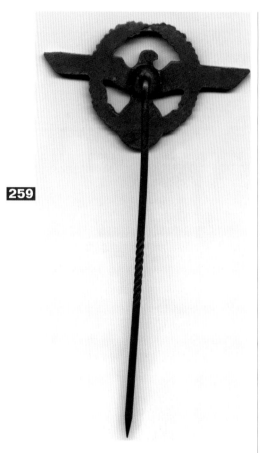

awards of this badge will be made on Workers' Day [1 May] 1937. The badge will be accompanied by a certificate and they will be presented by the local civilian manager or *Betriebsführer*.' Since this award was superseded by the Faithful Service Decoration for 25 Years' Service, introduced on 30 January 1938, the lifetime of the award was less than nine months and it is correspondingly rare. I have not seen a citation or a presentation case for this award.

Submarine (West France) Naval Shipyard Workers' Achievement Badge

Instituted: December 1943
Rarity: scarce
Known maker(s)/markings: unmarked

authorised by an order dated 14 July 1936. Later production badges were produced from white-coloured aluminium.

The scope of the badge was further extended by an order dated 1 October 1941, which made it compulsory for all non-uniformed civilian personnel of the armed forces to wear the badge. It was to be worn on and off duty in the occupied countries and in 'befriended countries', a somewhat double-edged sword, and on certain duties within the borders of the Reich. Thus, this seemingly insignificant badge had very broad terms of reference.

In April 1937 the German War Minister issued the following order: 'In pursuance of my directive of 30 April 1936, I ordain that all civilian workers and employees of the Army and Navy who have completed 25 years' service, will receive a golden badge. First

The design of this award incorporates a U-boat passing through a cogwheel, surmounted by a naval national eagle. A number of variations have been encountered in this award and can be broken down loosely into six distinct types. The differences, however, are not significant enough to be given individual categorisation. Suffice it to say that the collector should be aware of these variations and need not consider them important or as a reliable method of detecting a reproduction.

The cogwheel looks oval and resembles a bicycle tyre with a raised inner line and then a smooth portion running from it that slopes downwards to the outer edge. This is serrated, giving the impression of the teeth of the cogs. The stern of the U-boat runs under the left-hand portion of the cogwheel, as the viewer sees it, while the bow is superimposed over the right portion of the cogwheel. The conning

tower and periscope are positioned midway in the voided centre of the cogwheel and the deck gun just touches the left-hand inside of the cogwheel. At the apex of the cogwheel is positioned the naval national eagle, with the lower part of the wing just touching the top of the teeth. The swastika is superimposed across the cogwheel, with the upper arm on the bottom of the eagle's chest, while the tip of the lower arm just breaks the inner line of the cogwheel.

The reverse of the badge is plain and can be flat or semi-dished. The badge is produced in either bronze or fine zinc, as described in the table of variations below. In the case of the fine zinc, the badge is then bronzed. However, these badges subsequently lose their colour and give the impression of a silver badge, which gave rise to the theory that the badge existed in two grades, bronze and silver. This is not the case. The fine zinc variations are believed to have been produced in France for personnel employed in the bases there. The method of attachment was by a needle pin to the lapel of the civilian jacket.

Another form has been encountered, which is in silver-coloured metal. The U-boat in this case has no vents on its side, a larger deck gun and conning tower. There is no national emblem at the top of the cogwheel, which has plain serrations.

	1st	2nd	3rd	4th	G. Högel
Height of eagle	7mm	8mm	7mm	7mm	13mm
Length of wings	16.6mm	13.2mm	13mm	14mm	21mm
Height of cogwheel	18mm	16.5mm	18mm	18mm	30mm
Width of cogwheel	16mm	14.5mm	16mm	16mm	16mm
Height of U-boat	9mm	8mm	8mm	8mm	7mm
Length of U-boat	32mm	29.5mm	30mm	30mm	19mm
Total height	23.4mm	21mm	2mm	22mm	37mm
Length of pin	39mm	49mm	40mm	41mm	
Width of pin	2mm	2mm	2mm	2.5mm	
Weight of badge	4.1gm	4.1gm	3.4gm	3.6gm	4.25gm
Material	Bronze	Bronze	Fine Zinc	Fine Zinc	
Pin attachment	Soldered	Soldered	Riveted	Riveted	

To show the slight variations in the types, I have included them in tabular form for ease.

This little-known badge was first seen in an article published in the *Grüne Presse* (Green Press), dated 27 August 1944, and very little information has since come to light about it. It was apparently intended to recognise the efforts of the dockyard workers and technicians in the U-boat construction and repair programme. The article, which was accompanied by a photograph of the badge and three others of workers, made specific reference to the shipyard workers' badge (*Werftarbeiter Abzeichen*) being presented to submarine construction workers.

The award was introduced at the end of 1943, with the month presumed to be December. It was to reward dockyard workers and technicians who were servicing the U-boat fleet in Germany and the naval bases in occupied France. The citation indicates that the award was for one and a half years' service in the construction and repair of submarines. Whether it could be awarded to foreign workers in the service of the German Navy is not known.

The award was accompanied by a citation that read: 'Verleihungsurkunde, in Anerkennung vorbildlicher Leistung und Führung Während Seines Mehr Als 1 1/2 Jahre. Einsatzes im Westraum Verleihe Ich dem', followed by the position held and underneath, the name of the recipient. 'Mit Dieser Urkunde das Westwerftleistungsabzeichen', followed by the region of award, 'Den' and the date. Beneath is the signature of the awarding officer, his rank and position.

The protective packet or case, in which the badge was awarded, is unknown to the author.

Norway Destroyers Naval Shipyard Workers' Achievement Badge

Instituted: 1943
Rarity: extremely rare
Known maker(s)/markings: unmarked

This award is in the form of a cogwheel with a high-prowed destroyer passing through it. Surmounting the cogwheel is an open-winged eagle. The edge of the cogwheel is serrated to give the impression of teeth. The width across the teeth to the inner line is 4mm and the width across the cogwheel, tooth to tooth, is 16mm. The stern of the destroyer is positioned in the void between the third and fourth tooth and just protrudes past the edge of the tooth. On the ship's deck, adjacent to the inner edge of the right-hand side of the cogwheel, is positioned depth-charge apparatus. The ship's deck rises at the centre and on this is placed the superstructure and funnel.

262

Photo 262: Citations for the Norway Destroyers Naval Shipyard Worker's Achievement Badge. *John Robinson*

Photo 263: Norway Destroyers Naval Shipyard Worker's Achievement Badge.

Photo 264: Reverse of the Norway Destroyers Naval Shipyard Worker's Achievement Badge.

12 o'clock and completely obscures it, with the lower arm protruding below the inner line of the cogwheel. The whole design of the badge is silhouetted, work which is finely done by hand. The eagle measures 18mm across the wing tips and 10mm from the tip of the lower arm of the swastika to the crown of the eagle's head. The overall height of the badge is 22mm. The reverse is plain, with a 36mm soldered needle pin. The badge was produced in fine zinc and then bronzed.

The date of the introduction of the award is unknown, but it is possible that it was introduced in December 1943. The criteria for the award are unknown.

From the deck, adjacent to the bridge, runs an aerial which touches the inner edge of the cogwheel and runs over it, finishing at the underside of the eagle's wing. The aerial and a cross are superimposed on the cogwheel. The prow of the ship, with its gun, rises from the central deck line covering part of the cogwheel and just breaking the line of the teeth. The central area of the badge is voided. The height of the ship from waterline to the top of the funnel is 6mm and the width from stem to stern is 18mm.

The eagle that surmounts the cogwheel is of a particularly interesting design, as it appears to be flying straight up and to the viewer's right. Its wings are in an inverted V shape and its head looks upwards to the right. The fletching on the wing has an elongated upper raised line. Beneath this are four lines of pinfeathers and from these emanate two shorter lines of feathers, each of the straight lines being shorter than the one above. The eagle's chest is crosshatched to simulate fletching. In its talons it holds a raised swastika that is superimposed upon the tooth positioned at

LDO Numbers

During the early Nazi years, local dignitaries were able to produce all kinds of awards, which, in some instances, became elevated to official awards. Officially introduced awards, however, were strictly controlled from the Führer's chancellery and rigidly upheld by the *Leistungsgemeinschaft Deutscher Ordenshersteller* or Guild of German Order Manufacturers (abbreviated as LDO). Ministerialdirektor Heinrich Doehle was in charge of the 'Präsidial Kanzlei des Führers' in Berlin as well as its subsidiary branch the 'Ordenskanzlei'. This ministry allocated a supplier's or *Lieferant* number to those manufacturers who were awarded government contracts to make award pieces. Several firms were also authorised to manufacture awards for supply to the retail trade. Sales via this avenue were strictly controlled by the LDO, which can be considered very much a trade guild. The LDO ensured the maintenance of high quality and published information booklets to keep producers aware of new developments and production methods.

Firms authorised to manufacture pieces for private sale were allocated a *Herstellungszeichen*, or manufacturer's number, which was a numerical code prefixed by the letter L or more commonly L/. A few firms made both award and retail pieces. Such firms therefore had two identifying numbers. Far more firms were authorised to manufacture only official contract pieces than were authorised to manufacture retail sales copies. Each piece sold through an LDO approved retailer came with a small warranty card guaranteeing its quality and promising replacement of any faulty piece.

From March 1941, it was required by the organisation that the producers would stamp their L number to their products. The chancellery laid down the regulations and the

Photo 265: The Frontreif U-boat badge and Frontreif stick pin have always been controversial. Many collectors categorically believe they are fakes – I do not consider that anyone has seriously suggested these were worn by U-boat crews.

Photo 266: Reverse of the Frontreif U-boat badge. The theory is that these were commemoratives for the shipyard personnel who built the submarines. I have included the medal but consider it as a speculative entry.

LDO supervised their implementation. This seems somewhat confused, considering the L designation changed nearly annually from its introduction. Some firms entered the system being awarded an L number and then were either dropped or withdrew from the organisation, subsequently to be reinstated with a different L number. For some unexplained reason, some manufacturers were awarded multiple L numbers.

Photo 267: Badge for the entrance of the Torp.Kdo.Danzig.

Photo 268: Reverse for the entrance of the Torp.Kdo.Danzig badge.

Photo 269: Badge for the entrance of the Torp.Kdo.Danzig in another form.

Photo 270: Reverse for the entrance of the Torp.Kdo.Danzig badge in another form.

267

26:

LDO No	Company	Maker's mark	Location
1	Deschler & Sohn		München
2	C.E. Juncker	CEJ	Berlin
3	Wilhelm Deumer	WD	Lüdenscheid
4	Steinhauer & Lück	S & L	Lüdenscheid
5	Hermann Wernstein HW		Jena-Lobstedt
6	Fritz Zimmermann	FZS	Stuttgart
7	Paul Meybauer	PM	Berlin
8	Ferdinand Hoffstädter		Bonn/Rhein
9	Leifergsmeinschaft Pforzheimer Schmuckhandwerker		Pforzheim
10	Foerster & Barth		Pforzhiem
11	Grossmann & Co		Wien
12	Frank & Reif		Stuttgart-Zuffenhausen
13	Gustav Brehmer	GB	Markneukirchen/Sa.
14	L. Chr. Lauer	LN 1790	Nürnberg
15	Friedrich Orth	FO	Wien

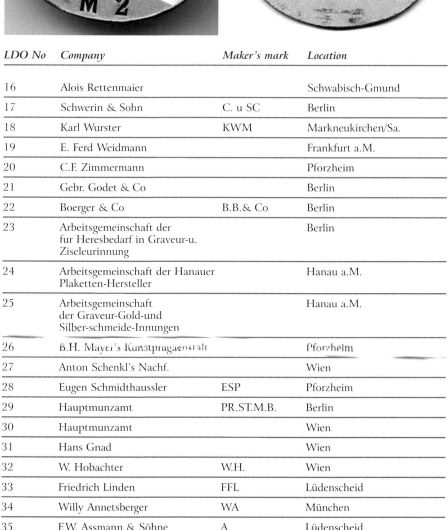

LDO No	Company	Maker's mark	Location
16	Alois Rettenmaier		Schwabisch-Gmund
17	Schwerin & Sohn	C. u SC	Berlin
18	Karl Wurster	KWM	Markneukirchen/Sa.
19	E. Ferd Weidmann		Frankfurt a.M.
20	C.F. Zimmermann		Pforzheim
21	Gebr. Godet & Co		Berlin
22	Boerger & Co	B.B.& Co	Berlin
23	Arbeitsgemeinschaft der fur Heresbedarf in Graveur-u. Ziseleurinnung		Berlin
24	Arbeitsgemeinschaft der Hanauer Plaketten-Hersteller		Hanau a.M.
25	Arbeitsgemeinschaft der Graveur-Gold-und Silber-schmeide-Innungen		Hanau a.M.
26	B.H. Mayer's Kunstprugaenstalt		Pforzheim
27	Anton Schenkl's Nachf.		Wien
28	Eugen Schmidthaussler	ESP	Pforzheim
29	Hauptmunzamt	PR.ST.M.B.	Berlin
30	Hauptmunzamt		Wien
31	Hans Gnad		Wien
32	W. Hobachter	W.H.	Wien
33	Friedrich Linden	FFL	Lüdenscheid
34	Willy Annetsberger	WA	München
35	F.W. Assmann & Söhne	A	Lüdenscheid
36	Bury & Leonhard		Hanau a.M.

LDO No	Company	Maker's mark	Location
37	Ad. Baumeister	Ad.B.L.	Lüdenscheid
38	Arbeitsgemeinschaft Metall und Kunstoff	AGMuK	Gablonz
39	Rudolf Bergs		Gablonz. a.d.N
40	Berg & Nolte	B & NL	Lüdenscheid
41	Gebr. Bender		Oberstein/Nahe
42	Beidermann & Co		Oberkassel b. Bonn
43	Julius Bauer Söhne		Zella Mehlis i. Thur
44	Jakob Bengel	JB. & Co	Idar/Oberdonau
45	Franz Jungwirth		Wien
46	Hans Doppler		Wels/Oberdonau
47	Erhard & Söhne AG		Schwabisch Gmund
48	Richard Feix		Gablonz a.d.N.
49	Josef Feix Söhne	JFS	Gablonz a.d.N.
50	Karl Gschiermeister		Wien
51	Eduard Gorlach & Söhne		Gablonz/N.
52	Gottleib & Wagner		Idar/Oberstein
53	Glaser & Söhne		Dresden

Photo 271: Shoulder board for GrandAdmiral.

Photo 272: Shoulder board for Admiral. *Tim Stannard collection*

Photo 273:
Shoulder board
for
Konteradmiral –
Admiral. *Tim
Stannard collection*

LDO No	Company	Maker's mark	Location
54	Gebrüder Wegerhoff	GWL	Lüdenscheid
55	J.E. Hammer & Söhne		Dresden
56	Robert Hauschild		Pforzheim
57	Karl Hensler		Pforzheim
58	Artur Jäkel & Co		Gablonz a.d.N.
59	Louis Keller		Oberstein
60	Katz & Deyhle		Pforzheim
61	Rudolf A. Karneth & Söhne	RK	Gablonz a.d.N.
62	Kerbach & Oesterhelt		Dresden
63	Franz Klamt & Söhne		Gablonz a.d.N.
64	Gottl. Fr. Keck & Sohn		Pforzheim
65	Klein & Quenzer AG	K. & Q.	Idar/Oberstein
66	Friedrich Keller		Oberstein
67	R. Kreisel	RK	Gablonz a.d.N.
68	Alfred Knoblock		Gablonz a.d.N.
69	Alois Klammer		Innsbruck
70	Lind & Meyrer		Oberstein a.d.N.
71	Rudolf Leukert		Gablonz a.d.N.
72	Franz Lipp		Pforzheim
73	Frank Mönert		Gablonz a.d.N.
74	Carl Meurer Sohn		Oberstein/Nahe
75	Franke & Co		Lüdenscheid
76	Ernst L. Muller		Pforzheim
77	Bayer. Hauptmunzamt		München

Photo 274:
Shoulder board for Korvettenkapitän. *Tim Stannard collection*

Photo 275:
Shoulder board on green underlay. *Tim Stannard collection*

LDO No	Company	Maker's mark	Location
78	Gustav Miksch		Gablonz a.d.N.
79	Matthias Kutsch	MK	Attendorn
80	G.H. Osang		Dresden
81	Overhoff & Cie	O & C	Lüdenscheid
82	Augustin Prager		Gablonz a.d.N.
83	Emil Peukert		Gablonz a.d.N.
84	Carl Posllath		Schrobenhausen
85	Julius Pietsch		Gablonz a.d.N.
86	Pulmann & Crone	P & CL	Lüdenscheid
87	Roman Palme		Gablonz a.d.N.
88	Werner Redo	W.R.	Saarlautern
89	Rudolf Richter	R.R.S.	Schlag 244 b. Gablonz
90	Aug. F. Richter K.G.		Hamburg
91	Josef Rössler & Co		Gablonz a.d.N.
92	Josef Rücker & Sohn		Gablonz a.d.N.
93	Richard Simm & Sohn	R.S. & S.	Gablonz a.d.N.
94	Ossenberg-Engels	OE	Iserlohn
95	Adolf Scholze		Grunwald a.d.N.
96	Robert Klein	RK	Wien

LDO No	Company	Maker's mark	Location
97	A.E. Köchert		Wien
98	Rudolf Souval	RS*	Wien
99	Schwertner & Cie		Graz-Eggenberg
100	Rudolf Wächtler & Lange		Mittweida i.Sa.
101	Rudolf Tham		Gablonz a.d.N.
102	Philipp Türks Ww.		Wien
103	Aug. G. Tham		Gablonz a.d.N.
104	Hein Ulbricht's Ww.		Kaufing b. Schwanenstadt
105	Heinrich Vogt		Pforzheim
106	Bruder Schneider AG	BSW	Wien
107	Carl Wild	CW	Hamburg
108	Arno Wallpach		Salzburg
109	Walter & Henlein	WH	Gablonz a.d.N.
110	Otto Zappe		Gablonz a.d.N.
111	Ziemer & Söhne		Oberstein
112	Argentor Werke Rust & Hetzel		Wien

* Contrary to what was a popularly held belief for many years, Rudolf Souval of Vienna used both angular and round forms of the letters on wartime products.

Photo 276:
Shoulder board on maroon underlay. *Tim Stannard collection*

Photo 277:
Shoulder board for Oberleutnant. *Tim Stannard collection*

LDO No	Company	Maker's mark	Location
113	Hermann Aurich	HA	Dresden
114	Ludwig Bertsch		Karlsruhe
115	Richard Sieper & Söhne	R.S.S.	Lüdenscheid
116	Funke & Brüninghaus	F & BL	Lüdenscheid
117	Hugo Lang		Wiesenthal a.N.
118	August Menzs & Sohn		Wiesenthal a.N.
119	Alfred Stübbe	AS in triangle	Berlin
120	Franz Petzl		Wien
121	Imme & Sohn	JMME	Berlin
122	J.J. Stahl		Strassburg
123	Beck, Hassinger & Co		Strassburg
124	Rudolf Schanes		Wien
125	Eugen Gauss		Pforzheim
126	Eduard Hahn	EH	Oberstein/Nahe
127	Moritz Hausch AG		Pforzheim
128	S. Jablonski GmbH		Posen
129	Fritz Kohm		Pforzheim
130	Wilh. Schröder & Co		Lüdenscheid
131	Heinrich Wander	W	Gablonz a.d.N.

LDO No	Company	Maker's mark	Location
132	Franz Reischauer		Idar-Oberstein
133			
134	Otto Klein	K in a circle	Hanau
135	Julius Möser		Oberstein
136	J. Wagner & Sohn		Berlin
137	J.H. Werner		Berlin
138	Julius Maurer	JMO	Oberstein
139	Hymmen & Co	H&CL	Lüdenscheid
140	Schauerte & Höhfeld		Lüdenscheid
141	Sohni, Heubach & Co	SH u Co	Oberstein
142	A.D. Schwerdt		Stuttgart
	Rath		München
	Rudolf Stübiger		Wien
	Otto Schickel		Pforzheim

Photo 278: Naval Chaplin right hand collar. *Tim Stannard collection*

Photo 279: Naval Chaplin left hand collar. *Tim Stannard collection*

Photo 280: M1942 pattern collar patch for Marine-oberpfarrer right hand collar. *Tim Stannard collection*

Photo 281: M1942 pattern collar patch for Marine-oberpfarrer left hand collar. *Tim Stannard collection*

Multiple LDO Numbers

The lists below are of manufacturers who had multiple L numbers. These L numbers apparently indicated full licences and part licences to produce certain state awards, such as the Iron Cross and Eagle Order. These two lists are interesting in that they both have 17 entries. Whether any intermediate listings are available is uncertain. These lists go some way towards supporting the theory that certain manufacturers produced parts and other manufacturers were engaged in the finishing of those medals. It is possible that these listings are relevant to that process. It is also possible that these numbers preceded the first list and that list is nothing more than an extension of these two lists.

LDO No	Company	Maker's mark	Location
L/10	Deschler & Sohn		München
L/11	Wilhelm Deumer	WD	Lüdenscheid
L/12	C.E. Juncker	CEJ	Berlin
L/13	Paul Meybauer	PM	Berlin
L/14	Friedrich Orth	FO	Wien
L/15	Otto Schickel		Pforzheim
L/16	Steinhauer & Lück	S & L	Lüdenscheid
L/17	Hermann Wernstein	HW	Jena-Lobstedt
L/18	B.H. Mayer Hofkunstprageanstalt		Pforzheim
L/19	Ferdinand Hoffstätter		Bonn/Rhein
L/20	Frank & Reif		Stuttgart
L/21	Foerster & Barth		Pforzheim
L/22	Rudolf Souval	RS*	Wien

282

28

L/23	Julius Maurer		Oberstein/Nahe
L/24	Fritz Zimmerman	FZS	Stuttgart
L/25	A.E. Kochert		Wien
L/26	Klein & Quenzer	K. & Q.	Oberstein/Nahe
L/50	Gebr. Godet & Co		Berlin
L/51	E. Ferd Weidmann		Frankfurt a.m.
L/52	C.F. Zimmermann		Pforzheim
L/53	Hymmen & Co		Lüdenscheid
L/54	Schauerte & Höhfeld		Lüdenscheid
L/55	Wächtler & Lange Rudolf		Mitweida i.Sa.
L/56	Funcke & Brüninghaus	F & BL	Lüdenscheid
L/57	Boerger & Co		Berlin
L/58	Glaser & Sohn		Dresden
L/59	Alois Rettenmaier		Schwabisch-Gmund
L/60	Gustav Brehmer	GB	Markneukirchen/Sa.
L/61	Friedrich Linden	FLL	Lüdenscheid
L/62	Werner Redo	W.R.	Saarlautern
L/63	G.H. Osang		Dresden
L/64	F.W. Assmann & Söhne	A	Lüdenscheid
L/65	Dr Franke & Co	KG	Lüdenscheid
L/66	A.D. Schwerdt		Stuttgart

Photo 282: M1942 pattern collar patch for Marine-dekan right hand collar. *Tim Stannard collection*

Photo 283: M1942 pattern collar patch for Marinedekan left hand collar. *Tim Stannard collection*

Photo 284: Instructors at the Marine – SA schools wore the dark blue-collar patch with a 4 cm gold anchor positioned in the centre at a 45-degree angle on the right hand collar patch of the Marine SA. *Tim Stannard collection*

Photo 285: Rank patch of the Marine SA. *Tim Stannard collection*

Photo 286: An interesting piece of personal attire: the unofficial admiral's stab in the form of a telescope as used by GrandAdmiral Karl Dönitz. The 23-inch-long baton was made from ebony in the form of a telescope. The body was bound in navy blue morocco leather, gilt embossed with fouled anchors, Wehrmacht eagles and iron crosses with copper gilt and silver roped boarder mounts. The screw on the top mount, which had possibly been an eagle and swastika, had been removed. The baton had come into the possession of one of the British intelligence officers who had interrogated the GrandAdmiral prior to the Nuremburg Trials.